MEDIA & POWER

GRAPHIC GUIDES
Series editor: Philip Boys

Anarchy
Clifford Harper

Apartheid
Donald Woods & Mike Bostock

Media and Power
Peter Lewis & Corinne Pearlman

Modern Art
Dave Clarke & Julie Hollings

Radiation and Health
Tony Webb & Robin Collingwood

Space Wars
Martin Ince & David Hine

Thatcher
Ed Harriman & John Freeman

Women Artists
Frances Borzello & Natacha Ledwidge

Forthcoming titles

Animal Liberation
Lori Gruen, Peter Singer & David Hine

The Birth of the Woman's Novel
Dale Spender & Natacha Ledwidge

Language and Power
Rob Pope & Graham Higgins

Logic and Power
Herb Kohl & Robin Collingwood

Revolutionary Women
Cathy Porter & Anna Louise

MEDIA & POWER
From Marconi to Murdoch
A GRAPHIC GUIDE

Peter M Lewis and
Corinne Pearlman

Camden Press

Published in 1986 by
Camden Press Ltd
43 Camden Passage, London N1 8EB, England
Text © Peter M Lewis
Illustrations © Corinne Pearlman
Designed by Corinne Pearlman

Set in Bodoni Roman
by Windhorse Photosetters
119 Roman Road, London E2 0QN

British Library Cataloguing in Publication Data
Lewis, Peter M.
Media & Power: from Marconi to Murdoch:
a Graphic Guide. – (Graphic guides)
1. Broadcasting – Social aspects 2. Broadcasting – History
I. Title   II. Series
302.2′344   HE8689.6
ISBN 0-948491-03-5

Printed by A. Wheaton & Co. Ltd., Exeter

Some of the images and text illuminating radio history
and community radio first appeared in Nos. 1 & 2 of
Relay magazine, 1981/2 (see 'Going Further', p.187).

CONTENTS

Introduction

BROADCASTING is in crisis, its traditional relations with government and audience threatened by media conglomerates commanding immensely powerful new technologies and multinational finance.

GOVERNMENTS have always claimed the right to control broadcasting, and the weapons they have had available to them – direct and indirect censorship, threats to withhold revenue and withdraw transmission licences, even the creation of moral panics about the dangers of unregulated television – have generally been sufficient to secure that control. For their part, broadcasters – especially those in the public service tradition – have been attentive to the desires of government and assumed the right to speak to and on behalf of whole nations. At the same time they have ignored or marginalised major sections of society. Audiences have had to make do with what they are given.

BUT THE OLD TRIANGLE of state, broadcasters and audience is now being challenged on both sides of the Atlantic by the consequences of a belief in an unregulated market. The resources at the disposal of some communications giants outweigh the gross national product of many countries. Reaching directly into the home with a combination of satellite, cable and video, such organisations can offer so much choice that the audiences on which broadcasting depended are breaking up. Put on the defensive, the broadcasters are shedding some services, raising a tariff on others, and substituting mass audience shows in the place of programmes hitherto directed at specific so-called 'minorities'.

AT TIMES like these, old mythologies about broadcasting's historical success in maintaining its 'independence' from sectional control, its 'traditions of public service', and its 'defence of the nation's culture' against subversion, foreign influence and commercial debasement, are wheeled out to justify the latest moves in the power struggle to rule the airwaves.

I N THIS BOOK we attempt to question such mythologies by offering a rather different version of history.

W E LOOK at the way broadcasting emerged in the Western world as a military-sponsored extension of wireless and telegraphy, and how, in the course of colonial and commercial expansion, radio and then TV have reflected and amplified the inequalities of wealth and power within and between nations. We also review some of the theories which attempt to assess what broadcasting does to our minds, but without forgetting that what we do with broadcasting may be no less significant.

S UCH an understanding of broadcasting's past and present is, we believe, of great importance. But we also argue that understanding is not enough – the point is to change it. We describe how certain groups and communities have shown how it is possible to contest the images of themselves in broadcast media and to challenge the way media decide what is important and what is not. Some have done this by working with existing stations – by, for instance, claiming a right of reply, making their own programmes, and securing better representation for their groups in the staffing of those stations. Others have set up radio or TV stations for themselves.

E ARLY in the story, the German playwright and poet Bertolt Brecht inveighed against the one-sided, one-way nature of existing broadcasting, and imagined a different development.

'Radio must be changed from a means of distribution to a means of communication. Radio would be the most wonderful means of communication imaginable in public life, a huge linked system. Would be, that is, if it were capable not only of transmitting but of receiving, of allowing the listener not only to hear but also to speak, and did not isolate the listener but brought about contact.'

A T CERTAIN times and places this dream has been realised. Our story celebrates these rare moments and suggests that there may still be time to reclaim the airwaves.

Chapter 1 FROM MARATHON TO MARCONI

For many thousands of years, communication over any distance was largely a matter of delivering physical messages in the form of speech or writing. Its speed was limited by the fastest available means of transport – runners or horses on land, ships by sea.

Coded signs – visual or auditory – were also possible. Between ships, for example, flag signals were developed. The British navy were good at this kind of thing, and by the battle of Trafalgar (1805) they had developed a code still in use to-day. Such signals were effective for simple messages…

RUNNERS BROUGHT NEWS OF GREEK VICTORY IN THE BATTLE OF **MARATHON**

IN AFRICA, MESSAGES WERE SENT BY DRUMBEAT

THE NORTH AMERICAN INDIAN PASSED ON NEWS BY **SMOKE SIGNAL**

IN THE SIXTEENTH CENTURY…

…**FIRES** WERE LIT BY THE ENGLISH TO WARN OF THE ARRIVAL OF THE SPANISH ARMADA.

except when commanders deliberately chose to confuse communications…

SIGNALS? I SEE NO SIGNALS!

COLOURED FLAGS TOLD NELSON'S FLEET: 'ENGLAND EXPECTS THAT EVERY MAN WILL DO HIS DUTY'.

WHAT'S THE FLAG FOR 'YOU MUST BE JOKING?'

THEY'RE STILL IN USE TODAY, ALONG WITH **SEMAPHORE**.

A B C D E F

NOTICE that telescope; it was important. Systems like naval flag codes or Chappe's telegraph couldn't work without the kinds of telescope that began to be manufactured towards the end of the 18th century. (*Tele-scope* = distance seeing, from the Greek.) **Claude Chappe** (1763-1805) invented a system of telegraphy (*tele-graph* = distance writing) first used in the French revolutionary war.

The two wooden arms could be arranged in any of 92 ways to refer to positions in Chappe's code-book, the first arm indicating the page number and the second the number of the word on that page.

By installing the apparatus on towers built at suitable intervals, signals could be sent the 450 miles from Paris to the fleet in Toulon in 20 minutes.

The British Admiralty soon got hold of the idea. Their version (they called it the Shutter Telegraph) could take orders from London to the fleet at Portsmouth (70 miles) in 15 minutes. (As we'll see time and again in our story, the need for fast communications at times of war has continued to be a major catalyst of technological innovation.)

But enhanced communications were crucial for other developments in the 19th century...

Empires were growing, colonies changing hands, trade routes needing to be secured. Nation-states were becoming more powerful, governments more centralised, and – in Britain especially – the Industrial Revolution was getting under way.

The need to transport raw materials and manufactured goods led to the development of **steam traction**. In 1825 the first passengers were carried on **George Stephenson's** Stockton to Darlington railway at a speed of 10mph. Flags, lamps and signals were not fast or efficient enough to ensure the necessary control and safety…

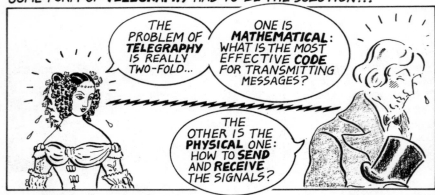

THE PROBLEM OF **TELEGRAPHY** IS REALLY TWO-FOLD...

ONE IS **MATHEMATICAL**: WHAT IS THE MOST EFFECTIVE **CODE** FOR TRANSMITTING MESSAGES?

THE OTHER IS THE **PHYSICAL** ONE: HOW TO **SEND** AND **RECEIVE** THE SIGNALS?

MON DIEU! 46 ET 59! SHE **LOVES** ME!

CHAPPE'S TELEGRAPH WAS **NOT** THE ONLY ANSWER...

AT THIS TIME, IN MANY COUNTRIES, BY A COMBINATION OF ACCIDENT AND PATIENT INVESTIGATION, PEOPLE WERE BEGINNING TO FIND WAYS OF USING **ELECTRICITY** AND **MAGNETISM** TO TRANSMIT SIGNALS AT A DISTANCE ALONG **WIRES**...

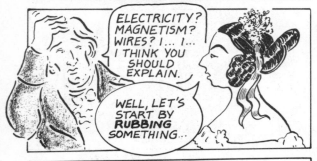

ELECTRICITY? MAGNETISM? WIRES? I... I... I THINK YOU SHOULD EXPLAIN.

WELL, LET'S START BY **RUBBING** SOMETHING...

FOR THOUSANDS OF YEARS, PEOPLE HAD KNOWN OF THE PHENOMENON OF **STATIC ELECTRICITY**. FOR EXAMPLE, THE GREEKS HAD NOTICED THAT AMBER (THE GREEK FOR AMBER IS 'ELEKTRON') WHEN RUBBED WITH A DRY WOOLLEN CLOTH, COULD MAKE SMALL SCRAPS OF STRAW DANCE.

GLASS, WHEN RUBBED WITH **SILK**, ACTED IN MUCH THE SAME WAY...

IN THE EIGHTEENTH CENTURY, STATIC ELECTRICITY, PRODUCED BY **FRICTION MACHINES**, WAS USED IN EXPERIMENTS...

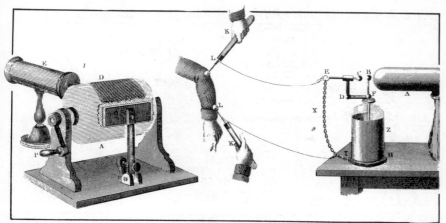

IN 1774 GEORGES **LESAGE** OF GENEVA BUILT A TELEGRAPH USING **WIRES** REPRESENTING EACH LETTER OF THE ALPHABET. THE WIRES RECEIVED **ELECTRIC IMPULSES** THROUGH A CONDUCTOR ATTACHED TO A **FRICTION MACHINE.**

BIT WHAT YOU MIGHT CALL **LABOUR-INTENSIVE...**

IN 1786 LUIGI **GALVANI** ACCIDENTALLY FOUND A WAY TO PRODUCE A **CONTINUOUS** FLOW OF CURRENT BY **CONTACTING DIFFERENT METALS...**

YES, AND HE USED OUR BODIES TO DETECT THE CURRENT...

IN 1800, HIS FRIEND ALESSANDRO **VOLTA** INVENTED THE ELECTRIC **BATTERY** OR 'VOLTAIC PILE' WHICH PRODUCED A MORE **PERMANENT** SOURCE OF CURRENT.

Zinc
Copper
Flannel
Soaked
in
brine

Live wire

THE NEXT SIGNIFICANT STEP WAS TO DISCOVER THE CONNECTION BETWEEN **ELECTRICITY** AND **MAGNETISM.**

+   −

IN 1820 HANS CHRISTIAN **OERSTED** DEMONSTRATED THAT A CURRENT FLOWING IN A WIRE COULD DEFLECT A COMPASS NEEDLE NEARBY. BY 1837 THE FIRST **ELECTRIC TELEGRAPH** HAD BEEN SET UP USING THIS DISCOVERY...

WILLIAM **COOKE** AND CHARLES **WHEATSTONE**, USING THE **FIVE-NEEDLE TELEGRAPH**, SHOWN HERE, SUCCESSFULLY SENT A SIGNAL FROM EUSTON TO CAMDEN TOWN.

THE DEVICE WAS RELATIVELY SIMPLE AND THE OPERATOR DIDN'T HAVE TO KNOW A CODE: HE READ OFF THE LETTER AT THE INTERSECTION OF THE TWO LINES DOWN WHICH THE NEEDLES POINTED (ONLY TWO MOVED AT A TIME).

IN BRITAIN, THE **GREAT WESTERN RAILWAY** WAS THE FIRST TO USE TELEGRAPHY ON ITS LINE BETWEEN **PADDINGTON** AND **SLOUGH** (A TELEGRAPH LINE TO NEARBY **WINDSOR** WAS HANDY FOR REPORTING **ROYAL NEWS**).

THE MAN WAS SPOTTED AT PADDINGTON, FOLLOWED, ARRESTED AND SUBSEQUENTLY CONVICTED.

THE TELEGRAPH RECEIVED SENSATIONAL PUBLICITY BECAUSE OF THIS EPISODE AND CAUGHT THE PUBLIC'S IMAGINATION. IN 1850 **PUNCH** CARRIED A PROPHETIC GLIMPSE OF THE FUTURE...

MUSIC BY ELECTRIC TELEGRAPH.

HANOVER SQUARE — PHIL HARMON — EXETER HALL

BUT **PUNCH** WAS NOT THE ONLY PROPHET. IN 1831 AN AMERICAN PORTRAIT PAINTER VISITING FRANCE HAD BEEN INTRIGUED BY CHAPPE'S TELEGRAPH...

THE MAILS IN OUR COUNTRY ARE TOO **SLOW**...

HE WROTE TO A FRIEND: "THIS FRENCH TELEGRAPH IS BETTER ... BUT EVEN **THIS** WILL NOT BE FAST ENOUGH. **THE LIGHTNING WOULD SERVE US BETTER**".

IT WAS ON HIS VOYAGE HOME ACROSS THE ATLANTIC THAT SAMUEL **MORSE** - FOR IT IS HE - WORKED OUT THE BASIS OF HIS FAMOUS DOT-DASH **CODE**, WHICH HIS FRIEND ALFRED VAIL WAS LATER TO HELP HIM PERFECT.

H M M M

	PRINTING.	SINGLE NEEDLE.		PRINTING.	SINGLE NEEDLE.
A	. —	✓/	N	— .	/\
B	— . . .	/\\\	O	— . —	///
C	— . — .	/\/\	P	. — — .	✓/\
D	— . .	/\\	Q	— — . —	//✓
E	.	\	R	. — .	✓/\
F	. . — .	\\/\	S	. . .	
G	— — .	//\	T	—	
H	. . . .	\\\\	U	. . —	
I	. .	\\	V	. . . —	
J	. — — —	✓///	W	. — —	
K	— . —	/\/	X	— . . —	
L	. — . .	✓/\	Y	— . — —	
M	— —	//	Z	— — . .	

THE MATHEMATICAL PROBLEM OF TELEGRAPHY— WHAT IS THE MOST EFFECTIVE CODE FOR TRANSMITTING MESSAGES— WAS NOW SOLVED. IN 1837 MORSE STAGED IN THE U.S.A. A DEMONSTRATION OF A SINGLE NEEDLE TELEGRAPH SYSTEM USING THE FIRST VERSION OF WHAT WAS LATER TO BECOME THE **INTERNATIONAL TELEGRAPH CODE**.

MORSE FINALLY WON THE BLESSING OF CONGRESS FOR THE LAYING OF A 40-MILE LINE BETWEEN WASHINGTON AND BALTIMORE. THE FIRST MESSAGE SENT DOWN IT ON MAY 24, 1844, GAVE THANKS FOR THE SUCCESS IN WORDS FROM THE BIBLE - **"WHAT GOD HATH WROUGHT!"**

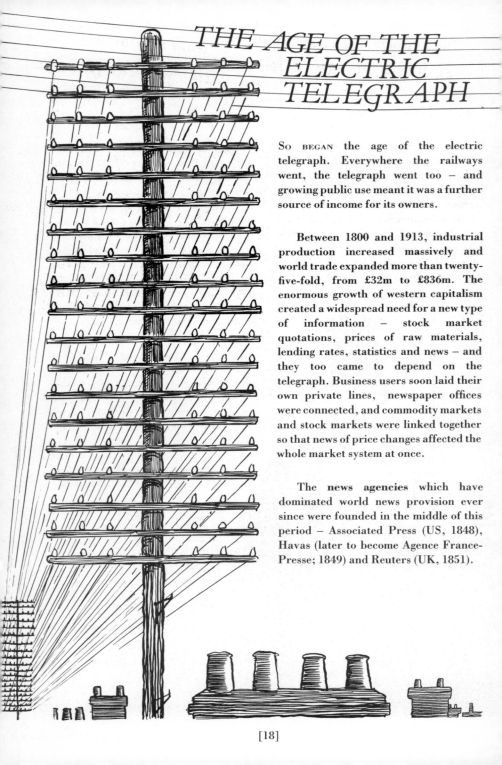

THE AGE OF THE ELECTRIC TELEGRAPH

So BEGAN the age of the electric telegraph. Everywhere the railways went, the telegraph went too – and growing public use meant it was a further source of income for its owners.

Between 1800 and 1913, industrial production increased massively and world trade expanded more than twenty-five-fold, from £32m to £836m. The enormous growth of western capitalism created a widespread need for a new type of information – stock market quotations, prices of raw materials, lending rates, statistics and news – and they too came to depend on the telegraph. Business users soon laid their own private lines, newspaper offices were connected, and commodity markets and stock markets were linked together so that news of price changes affected the whole market system at once.

The news agencies which have dominated world news provision ever since were founded in the middle of this period – Associated Press (US, 1848), Havas (later to become Agence France-Presse; 1849) and Reuters (UK, 1851).

The emergence of these various institutions demonstrates the important relationship between communications and business – the latter grows as the volume of information traffic increases. With continuous pressure to improve the speed and capacity of communication channels scientists and engineers were urged to overcome the new technical problems that arose.

In 1863, the British parliament passed its first measures to control the chaos produced by the many competing private telegraph companies and to ensure the priority of state business. The **Telegraphy Act** was important because it was the basis of all future attempts at state regulation of broadcasting. Nationalisation followed in 1868, placing telegraphs under the Post Office. By 1885, the network of post offices throughout Britain was handling 50 million telegrams a year.

At first, telegraph lines stopped at national frontiers. Operators copied down the messages and they were taken across the border for recoding and onward transmission. In 1849 Austria and Prussia signed a treaty to end this absurdity and link their telegraph systems. The treaty specified that government messages should come first, then railway ones. The public came last.

IF THEY *PAID* ME MORE *I'D* INVEST IN **GUTTA-PERCHA** - IT'S THE BEST INSULATION FOR THE **SUB-MARINE CABLES!**

Other countries imitated these arrangements but reaching across the sea was more difficult. The Atlantic Telegraph Co. bought £¼m worth of cable and spent large sums of money and five years of effort before successfully linking Europe with America. **Queen Victoria** inaugurated the line in 1858 by exchanging messages with the US President, **James Buchanan**. Her dedication, all 99 words of it, took 16½ hours to send.

Three months later the cable broke. In 1865 a new attempt, using **Brunel's** masterpiece *The Great Eastern* (the only ship large enough to carry the entire cable), ended in disaster when the cable slipped and was lost. However, in the following year it was able to retrieve the cable and put it into working order. In that same year, the **International Telegraphic Union** was established to regulate communications.

The submarine cables not only linked London to the colonial capitals of the British Empire – so that it was then and for the next half-century easier to call London from the capital of a distant colony than it was to make a call up-country or to a neighbouring (often rival) colony – but London became the hub of the business communications of the whole capitalist world.

THE **ATLANTIC TELEGRAPH** HAS HALF UNDONE THE DECLARATION OF 1776, AND HAS GONE FAR TO MAKE US ONCE AGAIN, IN SPITE OF OURSELVES, **ONE PEOPLE**.

CAPITAL BY ITS NATURE DRIVES BEYOND EVERY SPATIAL BARRIER. THUS THE CREATION OF THE PHYSICAL CONDITIONS OF EXCHANGE — OF THE MEANS OF COMMUNICATION AND TRANSPORT, THE ANNIHILATION OF SPACE BY TIME — BECOMES AN EXTRAORDINARY NECESSITY FOR IT.

KARL MARX, 1858

[21]

WITHIN a few years of the consolidation of telegraphy there was competition from another wonder — the telephone! 'Mr. Watson, please come here, I want you,' were the first words sent by **Alexander Graham Bell** in January 1875. Bell rushed round to the US Patent Office, beating another inventor, **Elisha Gray**, by two hours. (We'll hear more of these patent disputes later.)

In Britain, *The Times* was not impressed with this 'American Humbug'. Nor was **William Preece**, Electrician to the Post Office (later Engineer-in-Chief)...

I FANCY THE DESCRIPTIONS WE GET OF ITS USE IN AMERICA ARE A LITTLE EXAGGERATED. BUT THERE ARE CONDITIONS IN AMERICA WHICH NECESSITATE THE USE OF INSTRUMENTS OF THIS KIND MORE THAN HERE. HERE WE HAVE A **SUPERABUNDANCE** OF **MESSENGERS, ERRAND-BOYS** AND **OTHER THINGS OF THAT KIND**.

But Preece was wrong. The telephone was ideally suited to the growth of commerce. Without it, the huge business centres, office blocks and skyscrapers at the heart of cities would have been impossible.

IT **IS** RATHER **FAINT** AND ONE MUST HOLD THE TUBE CLOSE TO **ONE'S EAR**.

By the time **Guglielmo Marconi** came to Britain in 1896, the telephone and telegraph, together with the railways, were firmly established as the means of communication which supported the stage then reached by capitalism. But in the race to command the world market in raw materials on which economic expansion depended, the European powers began to dispute the ownership of the colonies they possessed.

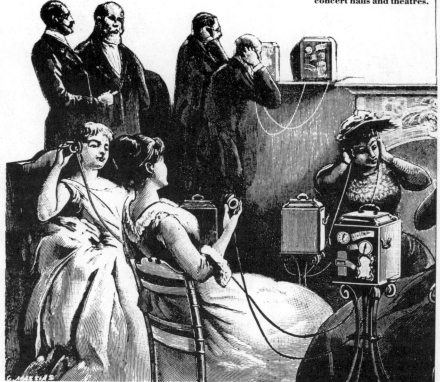

The telephone as entertainment: theatrophones in the lobby of a hotel in Paris connected guests to live performances in concert halls and theatres.

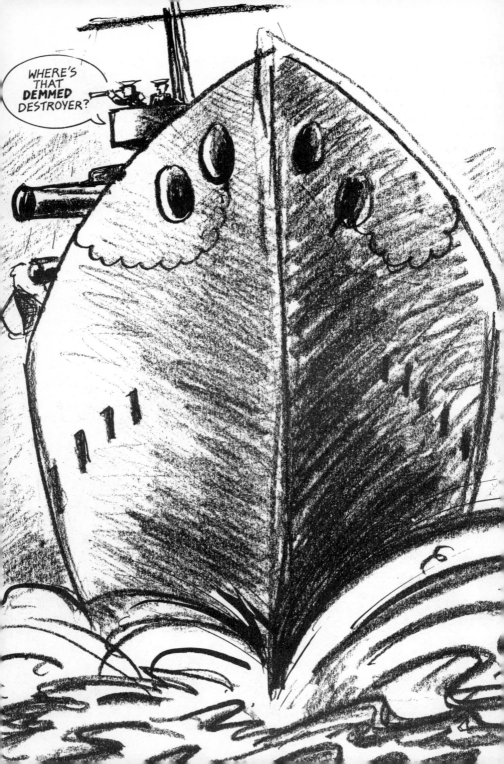

In this struggle, navies were crucial.

The arms race of the day involved the launching of ever-more heavily armoured and armed battleships, the answer to which was the smaller faster ship armed with the new torpedos, the answer to which was the torpedo-boat destroyer…

The speed of battle had now overtaken the ability to communicate. Ships' deployment and effectiveness were limited by the extent to which visible signals could be passed between them and between the fleet and the shore. On long voyages, ships were completely cut off.

**Something was needed,
and needed fast.**

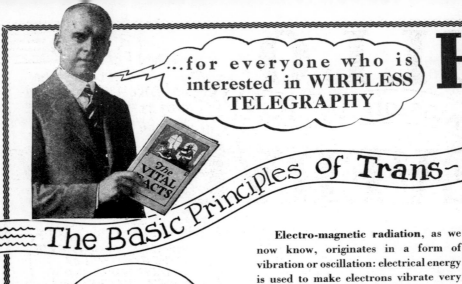

...for everyone who is interested in WIRELESS TELEGRAPHY

The VITAL FACTS

The Basic Principles of Trans-

H

IN 1864 I WAS THE FIRST TO **FORECAST** THE **EXISTENCE OF RADIO WAVES**

JAMES CLERK **MAXWELL**

Electro-magnetic radiation, as we now know, originates in a form of vibration or oscillation: electrical energy is used to make electrons vibrate very rapidly in the aerial circuit of a transmitter, and the energy applied is shed continuously as waves. Unlike sound, the waves produced do not require atmosphere in which to travel (so communication is possible through the vacuum of outer space). They travel for long distances and can penetrate where sound cannot.

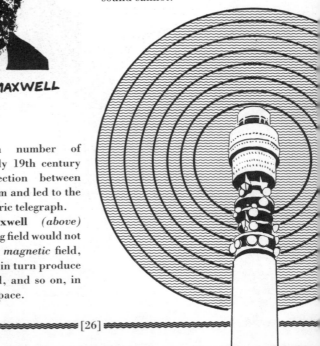

WE'VE seen how a number of experiments in the early 19th century established the connection between electricity and magnetism and led to the development of the electric telegraph.

James Clerk Maxwell *(above)* predicted that a vibrating field would not only induce a vibrating *magnetic* field, but that this field would in turn produce a vibrating *electric* field, and so on, in alternate waves across space.

ULLO

mission by RADIO WAVES

... those who AREN'T interested can re-join the NAVY at the end of this section.

EVERYBODY

Radio waves can be measured either by their *size* (wavelength)...

|WAVELENGTH|

... or by their *frequency* (the number of waves per second).

One vibration per second is known as a **Hertz** (abbreviated to **Hz**).

1 VIBRATION
A SECOND =
1 HERTZ

IN 1887 I WAS THE FIRST TO **DEMONSTRATE** THE **EXISTENCE OF RADIO WAVES** AND MY NAME HAS BEEN USED TO DESCRIBE THEIR **FREQUENCY**

HEINRICH **HERTZ**, PROFESSOR OF THEORETICAL PHYSICS AT KIEL UNIVERSITY

ELECTRO-MAGNETIC VIBRATIONS TRAVELLING AT THE SPEED OF LIGHT (300 MILLION METRES A SECOND)

The frequency of radio waves usually transmitted in broadcasting range from hundreds of vibrations per second to many millions per second. One thousand vibrations per second are called one kilohertz (1kHz), one million are one mega-Hertz (1MHz) and one thousand million are one giga-Hertz (1GHz).

For ease of reference, radio frequencies are arranged in **bands**, as follows:

Frequency	Hz	Waveband	Wavelength
Extremely low frequency (ELF)	(below 3kHz)	= Very long wave	(above 100km)
Very low frequency (VLF)	(3kHz-30kHz)	= Long wave	(100km-10km)
Low frequency (LF)	(30kHz-300kHz)	= Long wave	(10km-1km)
Medium frequency (MF)	(300kHz-3MHz)	= Medium wave	(1000m-100m)
High frequency (HF)	(3MHz-30MHz)	= Short wave	(100m-10m)
Very high frequency (VHF)	(30MHz-300MHz)		(10m-1m)
Ultra high frequency (UHF)	(300MHz-3GHz)	= Microwave	(1000mm-100mm)
Super high frequency (SHF)	(3GHz-30GHz)	= Microwave	(100mm-10mm)
Extra high frequency (EHF)	(30GHz-300GHz)	= Microwave	(10mm-1mm)

For simplicity, frequencies of radio waves are labelled from *low* to *high* and the corresponding wavelength from *long* to *short*. In other words, *long waves go with low frequencies* and *short waves go with high frequencies*.

In Britain today, **wavelength** is generally used as the label for stations in the long and medium wave band. Most British broadcasting services using medium wave are also assigned frequencies in the VHF band (a wasteful practice known as simulcasting). In this band, since wavelengths become inconveniently small to describe, **frequency** is the label.

The complete range of radio frequencies is known as the **radio-frequency spectrum**. Allocating frequencies is a matter of national and international regulation. Large areas are reserved for broadcasting, for radio navigation and for international telephone and telegraph communications. Much of the spectrum is hoarded by the police and military authorities... exactly *which* frequencies they use is classified information, but they may well be holding on to more than they need.

RADIO EXPLAINED

A station is allocated a particular frequency to transmit its signal. Before it carries any information a radio wave looks something like this:

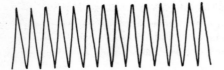

But how does it transmit *information* – a telegraph code, or sound, or pictures? To transmit sound or pictures, an electro-magnetic (radio)- wave has to have a *pattern* put on it (it has to be **modulated**). Once it carries this information it is called a **carrier wave**. Here we explain how the wave can be changed to carry *sound*.

Vibrating bodies make sounds, e.g. a guitar string when plucked.

Sound causes substances to vibrate, including *air*. Stronger sounds (e.g. thunder) cause stronger vibrations, so the size and frequency of the vibrations (or waves) vary with the strength of the sound. For instance, if you say 'hello', it may look like this:

A **microphone** converts *sound* vibrations into *electric* vibrations. There are many ways of doing this. Moving a wire near an electric magnet causes an electric current to flow in the wire. If a sound makes the wire vibrate, the electric current will vary with the strength of the vibrations.

So the current may look like this:

SOUND SIGNAL

It is this pattern which now has to be put onto the radio wave for transmission. There are two ways of doing it:

… by varying the *height* – the **amplitude** of the radio wave. This is known as **Amplitude Modulation** (AM) and it looks like this:

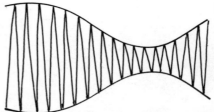

RADIO WAVE AFTER **AMPLITUDE MODULATION** – THE **HEIGHT** OF THE WAVE HAS BEEN VARIED TO REFLECT THE STRENGTH OF THE SOUND SIGNAL IT NOW CARRIES.

… or by varying the *frequency* of the radio wave so it looks like this:

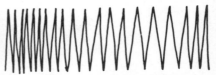

RADIO WAVE AFTER **FREQUENCY MODULATION (FM)** – THE **FREQUENCY** OF THE WAVE HAS BEEN VARIED TO REFLECT THE PATTERN OF THE SOUND SIGNAL

Since amplitude modulation is used by stations in the medium wave band, the terms medium wave and AM are often used as if synonymous. Since FM (frequency modulation) was first used for VHF transmissions, especially in the USA, FM and VHF are interchangeable terms in popular usage.

A radio wave that has been modulated to carry sound and pictures *takes up more space* on the frequency spectrum than if it were unmodulated.

The space taken up by the modulated wave is known as **bandwidth**. Speech, with relatively low frequency, occupies little bandwidth. Music takes up more, and pictures much more.

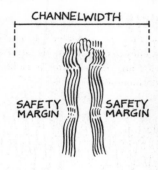

CHANNELWIDTH

SAFETY MARGIN   SAFETY MARGIN

Now let's go back to the 1890s, where we left some naval commanders unable to communicate with one another because of fog.

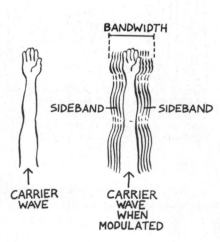

BANDWIDTH

SIDEBAND — — SIDEBAND

CARRIER WAVE

CARRIER WAVE WHEN MODULATED

WE'VE GOT A **BLOODY GOOD** NAVY AND A **BLOODY AWFUL** SIGNALLING SYSTEM. NOW WHAT ARE WE **BLOODY** GOING TO **DO** ABOUT IT?

To avoid interference, stations are allocated a safety margin each side of their bandwidth – this total width is known as **channelwidth** or simply a channel. Channels are a matter for national and international regulation.

At this time, and without any obvious connection, scientists in many parts of the world were busy improving on Hertz's experiments with electromagnetic waves. It fell to **Marconi**, whose story we now tell, to see the practical application of the scientific discoveries for the commercial and military needs of his day...

LIVORNO, 1887. MARCONI ENTERS THE TECHNICAL INSTITUTE..

MY PHYSICS LECTURES ARE SO EXCITING!

LATER...

I **MUST** LEARN MORE ABOUT ELECTRICITY AND MAGNETISM!

VERY WELL, MY SON. I WILL PAY FOR YOU TO HAVE EXTRA LESSONS.

THE MARCONIS' NEIGHBOUR, PROFESSOR RIGHI, HAD REPEATED HERTZ'S DEMONSTRATION OF RADIO WAVES (SEE PAGE 27) AND HAD IMPROVED THEIR TRANSMISSION WITH THE INVENTION OF HIS **OSCILLATOR**.

WHERE IS THAT BOY?

HE MUST BE WITH PROFESSOR RIGHI AGAIN.

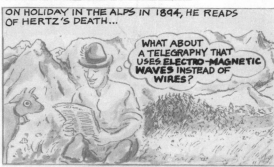

ON HOLIDAY IN THE ALPS IN 1894, HE READS OF HERTZ'S DEATH...

WHAT ABOUT A TELEGRAPHY THAT USES **ELECTRO-MAGNETIC WAVES** INSTEAD OF WIRES?

IN HIS ATTIC WORKSHOP MARCONI EXPERIMENTS WITH RADIO WAVES USING IMPROVEMENTS MADE SINCE HERTZ'S DAY, SUCH AS THE **COHERER**, OR SIGNAL DETECTOR, INVENTED BY PROFESSOR BRANLY, WHICH INCREASED THE SENSITIVITY OF RECEPTION. THIS WAS A SMALL GLASS TUBE CONTAINING LOOSE METAL FILINGS WHICH COHERED AND CONDUCTED AN ELECTRIC PULSE WHEN STRUCK BY A RADIO WAVE.

radio waves

metal plate

coherer

metal plate

battery

bell

BY THE END OF 1894...

WE DEMAND A DEMONSTRATION, COUSIN!

WHEN I PRESS THIS KEY THE BUZZER SOUNDS...

BUT YOU'RE NOT USING ANY WIRES!

BY CHANCE, MARCONI FOUND THAT WHEN HE ADJUSTED THE TWO METAL PLATES ATTACHED TO HIS APPARATUS BY RAISING ONE INTO THE AIR AND BURYING THE OTHER INTO THE EARTH, HE COULD IMPROVE THE DISTANCE OF TRANSMISSION. HE HAD DISCOVERED THE POWER OF RADIATION FROM AN AERIAL AND EARTH SYSTEM.

FINALLY...

BANG

D-DRING!

I MUST LET GUGLIELMO KNOW WE'VE RECEIVED HIS SIGNAL

IT MUST HAVE COME *THROUGH* THE HILL, SIR.

...OR WAS IT GOING *OVER* THE HILL. IT WAS STILL TOO EARLY TO SAY.

NOW HE WAS READY TO GO PUBLIC.

THE MINISTRY OF POSTS AND TELEGRAPHS AREN'T INTERESTED IN MY INVENTION.

VERY WELL... PERHAPS THE *BRITISH* WILL BE. WE SHALL STAY WITH MY RELATIVES.

BUT AT THE CUSTOMS...

YOU CAN'T BE TOO CAREFUL.

H.M. CUSTO

ITALIAN ANARCHISTS!

NOT ONE TO BE DAUNTED, MARCONI REBUILT HIS 'BLACK BOX', FILED A PATENT AND GOT AN INTRODUCTION TO THE CHIEF ENGINEER OF THE POST OFFICE, WILLIAM ("WE'VE GOT ERRAND BOYS") PREECE.

A SUCCESSFUL DEMONSTRATION TOOK PLACE ON 27 JULY 1896 WHEN MARCONI SENT SIGNALS BETWEEN TWO POST OFFICE BUILDINGS IN THE HEART OF THE CITY OF LONDON.

YOUNG MAN, YOU HAVE DONE SOMETHING TRULY EXCEPTIONAL. I CONGRATULATE YOU ON IT.

PREECE SECURED POST OFFICE AND WAR OFFICE BACKING, AND FURTHER TRIALS FOLLOWED ON SALISBURY PLAIN AND ACROSS THE BRISTOL CHANNEL.

SUDDENLY MARCONI WAS ALL THE RAGE...

JUST LISTEN TO THIS! "YOUR WAVES, DEAR SIR, MAKE MY FEET TICKLE!"

THE CALM OF MY LIFE HAS ENDED!

MARCONI'S NATIVE ITALY WAS NOT SO POPULAR... IN 1896 SHE HAD SUFFERED A MAJOR DEFEAT BY THE ABYSSINIANS (NOW ETHIOPIANS) IN ATTEMPTING TO ADD ERITREA TO HER COLONIES.

Ouch!

YOU CAN'T KICK *US* OUT OF ERITREA!

ERITREA

ABYSSINIA

ITALY, A YOUNG NATION, WAS ANXIOUS NOT TO LOSE A FAMOUS CITIZEN AS WELL.

MORE NEWS FROM ABROAD OF MARCONI'S SUCCESS!

OUR PAST LACK OF INTEREST MAY BE ENGLAND'S FUTURE GAIN. HE HAS ALREADY DEFERRED MILITARY SERVICE.

THE GOVERNMENT MADE AMENDS BY NOMINALLY APPOINTING MARCONI ASSISTANT NAVAL ATTACHÉ TO THEIR EMBASSY IN LONDON, SO THAT HE COULD CONTINUE HIS WORK.

LATER HE WAS CALLED HOME TO DEMONSTRATE HIS INVENTION. IN TRIALS AT LA SPEZIA, SIGNALS WERE RECEIVED FROM THE WARSHIP 'SAN MARTINO' WHEN THE VESSEL WAS BEYOND THE HORIZON.

ARRIVA MARCONI!

BRAVO!

BUT THE SIGNALS CAME *THROUGH* THE WATER!

SCIENTISTS OF THE TIME COULD NOT EXPLAIN THIS...

SURELY, ELECTRO-MAGNETIC WAVES FOLLOW A STRAIGHT LINE, LIKE LIGHT.

MARCONI WAS SOMEHOW PROVING THAT THE WAVES WERE BEING CONDUCTED *ROUND* THE EARTH. IT SEEMED THAT POTENTIALLY THERE WAS NO LIMIT TO THE DISTANCE THAT RADIO WAVES COULD COVER.

BACK IN LONDON, THE MARCONI WIRELESS AND SIGNAL COMPANY HAD BEEN FORMED TO DEVELOP HIS PATENTS...

SUCH A COMMERCIAL CONCERN DOES NOT EXIST SOLELY FOR THE PURPOSE OF SECURING A PECUNIARY RETURN TO THOSE WHO HAVE BRAVED RISKS...

MARCONI SET UP EXPERIMENTAL WIRELESS STATIONS IN THE ISLE OF WIGHT AND LATER AT POOLE...

WE'LL NEED TO DRILL A HOLE IN THIS WINDOW-PANE!

HOPE THE HOTEL MANAGEMENT DON'T MIND!

NONSENSE! THESE TRIALS ARE BRINGING IN GUESTS BY THE HUNDRED!

MARCONI'S LOVE OF SAILING AND HIS UNERRING INSTINCT FOR PUBLICITY LED HIM, IN 1898, TO THE FOCAL POINT OF FASHION AND NEWSPAPER ATTENTION— THE SUMMER REGATTA SEASON. THE *DUBLIN DAILY EXPRESS* COMMISSIONED HIM TO REPORT BY WIRELESS ON THE KINGSTOWN YACHT RACES. THIS FIRST-EVER USE OF WIRELESS BY THE PRESS WAS SEEN 'AS A TEST OF THE COMMERCIAL VALUE OF THE MARCONI SYSTEM' (THE TIMES).

IT PROVED A BRILLIANT AND WELL-PUBLICISED SUCCESS AND LED TO AN INVITATION FROM QUEEN VICTORIA TO SET UP WIRELESS COMMUNICATION BETWEEN HER RESIDENCE ON THE ISLE OF WIGHT...

... AND THE ROYAL YACHT, MOORED TWO MILES AWAY IN THE SOLENT, WHERE THE PRINCE OF WALES WAS ENTERTAINING FRIENDS WHILE CONVALESCING FROM A KNEE INJURY.

OH NO! NOT *ANOTHER* MESSAGE FROM MAMMA!

ONE DAY, MARCONI REFUSED TO LEAVE THE GARDEN WHILE THE QUEEN WAS OUT WALKING IN HER BATHCHAIR...

GET ANOTHER ELECTRICIAN!

ALAS, YOUR MAJESTY.... ENGLAND HAS NO MARCONI!

IN 1899 THE *NEW YORK HERALD* COMMISSIONED MARCONI TO COVER THE AMERICAS CUP...

... AND THE RETURN OF A TRIUMPHANT UNITED STATES NAVY FROM THE SPANISH-AMERICAN WAR. FLUSHED WITH ITS FIRST TASTE OF IMPERIALIST ADVENTURE, THE U.S.A. HAD ACQUIRED CUBA, GUAM, PUERTO RICO, HAWAII AND THE PHILIPPINES IN 1898, THANKS TO 'THE SPLENDID LITTLE WAR' IN WHICH THOUSANDS LOST THEIR LIVES.

THE YEAR BEFORE, THEODORE ROOSEVELT, THEN ASSISTANT SECRETARY TO THE NAVY, HAD SAID:

"WE MUST HAVE A GREAT NAVY... AN ARMAMENT FIT FOR THE NATION'S NEEDS, NOT PRIMARILY TO FIGHT, BUT TO AVERT FIGHTING ...

"PREPARATION FOR WAR IS THE SUREST GUARANTY FOR PEACE".

NOW THE U.S. NAVY WAS INTERESTED IN TESTING MARCONI'S APPARATUS...

BUT THESE MESSAGES ARE UNINTELLIGIBLE!

WE'RE GETTING SIGNALS FROM TWO SOURCES!

HMMPH! IF HE CAN'T TUNE OUT UNWANTED SIGNALS...

ONLY TWO SHIPS AT A TIME CAN EXCHANGE MESSAGES!

BUT THE AVERAGE FLEET MANOUEVRE REQUIRES MORE COMPLICATED EXCHANGES!

IN FACT, I'D WORKED OUT IN *THEORY* HOW TO STOP INTERFERENCE, BUT HADN'T YET DEMONSTRATED IT IN *PRACTICE*. WITHOUT A PATENT, I *CERTAINLY* WASN'T PREPARED TO EXPLAIN IT TO THE U.S. NAVY!

LATER, MARCONI'S PATENT 7777 OF 1900 SHOWED HOW INTERFERENCE COULD BE AVOIDED BY ATTUNING RECEIVER AND TRANSMITTER TO THE SAME FREQUENCY.

SOON...

THE COMPANY HAS SO MANY CLIENTS NOW, GUGLIELMO, BESIDES THE BRITISH NAVY.

LLOYD'S NEEDS EARLY NEWS OF THE SAFE ARRIVAL OR OTHERWISE OF ITS INSURED CARGOES... AND THERE'S TRINITY HOUSE, THE LIGHTSHIP ORGANISATION.

AND WHEN A STEAMER RAN INTO A LIGHTSHIP SUPPLIED WITH MARCONI'S EQUIPMENT...

THE FIRST SEA RESCUE THROUGH WIRELESS TOOK PLACE IN 1899.

BUT IN SOUTH AFRICA, WHERE THE BRITISH WERE FIGHTING THE BOERS...

WE'LL **NEVER** GET THIS WIRELESS TO WORK!

HMMPH! THESE KITES DON'T KEEP THE AERIALS UP....

...THE FIVE MOBILE STATIONS ORDERED BY THE ARMY FOR THE BOER WAR PUT UP A POOR PERFORMANCE —

THE WAR OFFICE FAILED TO PROVIDE MY MEN WITH SUITABLE MASTS...

SO THEY WERE REMOVED AND PUT ON NAVY SHIPS INSTEAD, THANKS TO:

CAPTAIN JACKSON, RN

I HOPE IT WILL ENABLE ME TO DO SUCCESSFULLY THAT FOR WHICH I WANT A FORCE THREE TIMES AS LARGE WITHOUT IT.

MARCONI WAS AFTER LONG DISTANCE, POINT-TO-POINT COMMUNICATIONS BY WIRELESS TELEGRAPHY.

I AM DETERMINED TO SPAN THE ATLANTIC WITH A WIRELESS MESSAGE!

IT CAN'T BE DONE!

SURELY, ELECTRO-MAGNETIC WAVES CANNOT PENETRATE THE 'HORIZON' BETWEEN ENGLAND AND AMERICA!

YEARS LATER, MARCONI SAID:-

LONG EXPERIENCE HAS TAUGHT ME NOT ALWAYS TO BELIEVE IN THE LIMITATION INDICATED BY PURELY THEORETICAL CONSIDERATIONS OR EVEN BY CALCULATIONS.

IN FACT, AS WE **NOW** KNOW, LONG WAVES ARE CONDUCTED **ROUND** THE EARTH'S SURFACE, OR **REFLECTED** BETWEEN THE LAND OR SEA AND THE **IONOSPHERE**...

MARCONI DIDN'T KNOW THIS BUT...
THE IONOSPHERE IS COMPOSED OF SEVERAL LAYERS, THE LOWEST OF WHICH IS ABOUT 85 KILOMETRES ABOVE THE EARTH'S SURFACE. DURING DAYLIGHT HOURS, THE LONGER WAVELENGTHS ARE **ABSORBED** BY THIS LOWEST LAYER.

WHEN DARKNESS COMES AND THE SUN'S RAYS LEAVE THE LOWEST LAYER, IT DISAPPEARS. NOW THE HIGHER LAYERS OF THE IONOSPHERE ARE EXPOSED AND THESE *REFLECT THE WAVES BACK TO EARTH*, GREATLY INCREASING THEIR RANGE AND CAUSING THAT *BABEL* YOU CAN HEAR ON YOUR RADIO ON MEDIUM WAVE AT NIGHT.

The First Trans-

Glace Bay, Newfoundland

IN 1901, STATIONS WERE BUILT AT POLDHU IN CORNWALL AND AT CAPE COD IN THE U.S.A.

STORMS BLEW DOWN THE HUGE STRUCTURES BUILT TO CARRY THE AERIALS. MARCONI HAD THE CORNISH STATION REBUILT IN A WEEK TO A SIMPLER DESIGN AND REMOVED THE U.S. STATION TO A NEARER SITE AT ST. JOHN'S, NEWFOUNDLAND, SOME 1800 MILES AWAY.

HERE, IN BITTER WINTRY WEATHER, WITH ASSISTANTS KEMP AND PAGET (AS SEEN ABOVE), MARCONI USED A BALLOON AND KITES TO RAISE AN AERIAL, WITH WHICH HE HOPED TO **RECEIVE IN MORSE CODE** **THE LETTER 'S' (THREE DOTS)** THAT HE'D ARRANGED TO BE TRANSMITTED FROM CORNWALL.

ON THURSDAY, DECEMBER 12, MARCONI RECEIVED THE FIRST SIGNALS.

THE WEATHER WORSENED AND HE DECIDED TO ABANDON THE EXPERIMENT, CONVINCED HE HAD DONE ENOUGH TO PROVE THE PRACTICABILITY OF A TRANS-ATLANTIC SERVICE.

Transmitter
Ionosphere
DAY-TIME
Receiver

Transmitter
NIGHT-TIME
Receiver

(THE RANGE OF LONG AND MEDIUM WAVES IS GREATLY INCREASED AT NIGHT)

Atlantic Message

Poldhu, Cornwall

MARCONI WAS HASTENED ON HIS WAY BY AN INJUNCTION SERVED BY THE *ANGLO-AMERICAN TELEGRAPH COMPANY* WHO CLAIMED HE WAS INFRINGING THEIR MONOPOLY ON WIRELESS TELEGRAPHY WITHIN THE COLONY OF NEWFOUNDLAND.

ALTHOUGH SOME PEOPLE DOUBTED MARCONI'S CLAIM TO HAVE HEARD THE MORSE SIGNAL (**"ONE SWALLOW DOES NOT MAKE A SUMMER, AND A SERIES OF 'S' SIGNALS DO NOT MAKE THE MORSE CODE"** SAID ONE NEW YORK CRITIC), HE HAD GENEROUS SUPPORT FROM A TOP SCIENTIST WHOSE SKILL IN ORGANISING RESEARCH AND MANIPULATING PATENT LAWS HAD FENCED OFF HUGE AREAS OF MODERN COMMUNICATIONS FOR HIS COMPANY (THE ELECTRIC LIGHT BULB, THE PHONOGRAPH, CINEMATOGRAPHY):

"I'M GLAD HE DID IT! THAT FELLOW'S WORK PUTS HIM IN MY CLASS. IT'S A GOOD THING WE CAUGHT HIM YOUNG!"

THOMAS EDISON

[39]

The Imperial

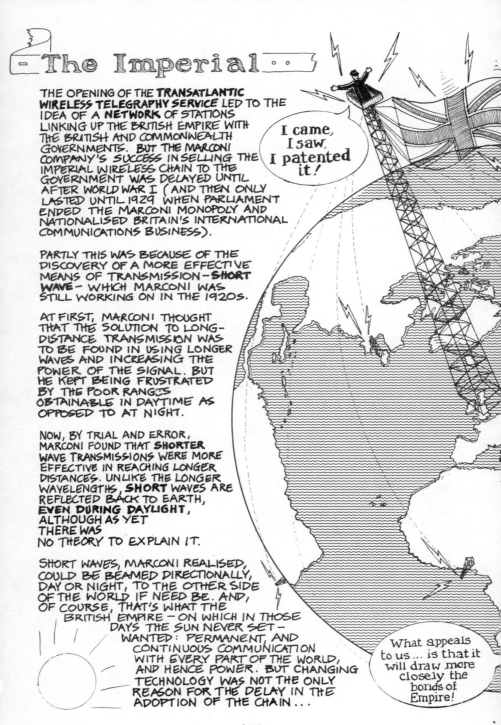

THE OPENING OF THE **TRANSATLANTIC WIRELESS TELEGRAPHY SERVICE** LED TO THE IDEA OF A **NETWORK** OF STATIONS LINKING UP THE BRITISH EMPIRE WITH THE BRITISH AND COMMONWEALTH GOVERNMENTS. BUT THE MARCONI COMPANY'S SUCCESS IN SELLING THE IMPERIAL WIRELESS CHAIN TO THE GOVERNMENT WAS DELAYED UNTIL AFTER WORLD WAR I (AND THEN ONLY LASTED UNTIL 1929 WHEN PARLIAMENT ENDED THE MARCONI MONOPOLY AND NATIONALISED BRITAIN'S INTERNATIONAL COMMUNICATIONS BUSINESS).

PARTLY THIS WAS BECAUSE OF THE DISCOVERY OF A MORE EFFECTIVE MEANS OF TRANSMISSION – **SHORT WAVE** – WHICH MARCONI WAS STILL WORKING ON IN THE 1920s.

AT FIRST, MARCONI THOUGHT THAT THE SOLUTION TO LONG-DISTANCE TRANSMISSION WAS TO BE FOUND IN USING LONGER WAVES AND INCREASING THE POWER OF THE SIGNAL. BUT HE KEPT BEING FRUSTRATED BY THE POOR RANGES OBTAINABLE IN DAYTIME AS OPPOSED TO AT NIGHT.

NOW, BY TRIAL AND ERROR, MARCONI FOUND THAT **SHORTER** WAVE TRANSMISSIONS WERE MORE EFFECTIVE IN REACHING LONGER DISTANCES. UNLIKE THE LONGER WAVELENGTHS, **SHORT** WAVES ARE REFLECTED BACK TO EARTH, **EVEN DURING DAYLIGHT**, ALTHOUGH AS YET THERE WAS NO THEORY TO EXPLAIN IT.

SHORT WAVES, MARCONI REALISED, COULD BE BEAMED DIRECTIONALLY, DAY OR NIGHT, TO THE OTHER SIDE OF THE WORLD IF NEED BE. AND, OF COURSE, THAT'S WHAT THE BRITISH EMPIRE – ON WHICH IN THOSE DAYS THE SUN NEVER SET – WANTED: PERMANENT, AND CONTINUOUS COMMUNICATION WITH EVERY PART OF THE WORLD, AND HENCE POWER. BUT CHANGING TECHNOLOGY WAS NOT THE ONLY REASON FOR THE DELAY IN THE ADOPTION OF THE CHAIN ...

I came, I saw, I patented it!

What appeals to us ... is that it will draw more closely the bonds of Empire!

MEANWHILE, ON THE HIGH SEAS...

WIRELESS WAS MAKING NEWS — AND MARCONI'S REPUTATION!

A MAN WANTED FOR MURDER, **DR. CRIPPEN**, ESCAPING IN DISGUISE WITH HIS MISTRESS ABOARD THE **S.S. MONTROSE**, WAS SPOTTED BY THE CAPTAIN WHOSE WIRELESS MESSAGE TO SCOTLAND YARD ENABLED **'MR. ROBINSON'** TO BE ARRESTED ON ARRIVAL IN QUEBEC. (THE CAPTAIN ALSO SENT EXCLUSIVE DISPATCHES TO THE **DAILY MAIL** WHOSE READERS WERE REGALED WITH DETAILED DESCRIPTIONS OF CRIPPEN'S LIFE DURING THE VOYAGE).

WHEN THE **TITANIC** STRUCK AN ICEBERG IN APRIL 1912, THOUGH THERE WAS DREADFUL LOSS OF LIFE, **NO-ONE** WOULD HAVE SURVIVED IF THE **CARPATHIA** HAD NOT PICKED UP THE TITANIC'S DISTRESS CALLS. THE NEW **S.O.S** WAS TRANSMITTED FOR THE FIRST TIME, ALONG WITH THE OLD **C.Q.D.** — COME QUICK DANGER!

PURE INDIAN TEA

BRITAIN'S BEST BEVERAGE

No. 5,677.]

Weekly Dispatch

109TH YEAR

SUNDAY, JULY 31, 1910.

SUNDAY SPECIAL EDITION

CRIPPEN'S LIFE AT SEA DESCRIBED BY 'WIREL

DETECTIVE INSᵀᴿ DEW

Mᴿˢ CRIPPEN — (MISS BELLE-ELMORE).

H.H.Crippen.

THE DOCTOR'S FIRST WIFE Mᴿˢ CHARLOTTE CRIPPEN

RIPPEN'S LIFE AT SEA

The New York Times.

THE WEATHER.

ONE CENT

745 SAW TITANIC SINK WITH 1,595, HER BAND PLAYING; HIT ICEBERG AT 21 KNOTS AND TORE HER BOTTOM OUT; 'I'LL FOLLOW THE SHIP,' LAST WORDS OF CAPT. SMITH. MANY WOMEN STAYED TO PERISH WITH HUSBANDS

THRILLING STORY BY TITANIC'S SURVIVING WIRELESS MAN

Bride Tells How He and Phillips Worked and How He Finished a Stoker Who Tried to Steal Phillips's Life Belt   Ship Sank to Tune of "Autumn"

Rescue Ship Arrives
Thousands Gather At the Pier.

FOUR BODIES BROUGHT IN

206 of the Crew and 4 Officers Are Among Those Rescued.

THREE LIFEBOATS LOST

Two Filled with Women Were Drawn Under and One Was Swamped.

Col. Astor Went Down Waving Farewells to His Bride.

SOME STORIES OF PANIC

SHOCK CALLED "SLIGHT JAR"

Card Playing Continued in the Cabin and None Realized the End Was Near.

SOME HEARD SHOTS FIRED

A False Rumor of Captain's Suicide and Shooting of Man Rushing for Boats.

BY HAROLD BRIDE, SURVIVING WIRELESS OPERATOR OF THE TITANIC.

THE **MILITARY** SAW IN WIRELESS TELEGRAPHY A GREATLY INCREASED POTENTIAL FOR IMPROVING THEIR COMMAND AND CONTROL SYSTEMS. AND IMPERIALIST WARS GAVE THEM PLENTY OF OPPORTUNITY FOR TESTING THE NEW DEVICE — AS WE HAVE SEEN, THE BRITISH AGAINST THE BOERS IN SOUTH AFRICA, (1899–1902), AND THE RUSSIANS AND JAPANESE AT WAR OVER MANCHURIA (1904–5).

GOTCHA, TELEFUNKEN!!

IN 1911, ITALY, ENCROACHING ON THE AILING OTTOMAN EMPIRE, FOUGHT THE TURKISH ARMY IN THE LIBYAN DESERT. MARCONI, ON THE ITALIAN WARSHIP *PISA*, WATCHED THE GUNS WRECKING THE TURKISH POSITIONS, INCLUDING THEIR GERMAN-SUPPLIED TELEFUNKEN EQUIPMENT.

IN 1905, THE JAPANESE, WITH MARCONI EQUIPMENT ON THEIR SHIPS, TOTALLY DESTROYED, FIRST, RUSSIA'S PACIFIC FLEET, AND THEN HER ATLANTIC FLEET, SENT ALL THE WAY ROUND AFRICA TO REPLACE IT.

AT THE OUTBREAK OF THE **FIRST WORLD WAR**, THE BRITISH ADMIRALTY ASSUMED CONTROL OF THE MARCONI WORKS. THE COMPANY'S WIRELESS TELEGRAPHISTS ACTED AS OPERATORS AND TRAINING OFFICERS FOR THE ARMED FORCES AND MERCHANT NAVY. **AIR-TO-GROUND TELEGRAPHY** AND **DIRECTION-FINDING** TECHNIQUES, BOTH INITIATED BEFORE THE WAR, WERE MADE OPERATIONALLY EFFECTIVE.

WITH ITALY OPPOSING GERMANY AND AUSTRIA-HUNGARY, MARCONI HIMSELF SERVED AS A MAJOR IN THE ITALIAN ENGINEERS, INSPECTING MOBILE WIRELESS STATIONS.

WHEN THE USA ENTERED THE WAR IN 1917, MARCONI, AS HIS COUNTRY'S MOST FAMOUS CITIZEN, REPRESENTED ITALY ON A MISSION TO DISCUSS FINANCE WITH THE NEW ALLY.

WE WANT MARCONI!

NOT **ANOTHER** SPEECH! THIS IS EXHAUSTING!

FOR A WHILE HE WAS BUSY WITH POLITICS AND DIPLOMACY. AFTER THE WAR HE WAS APPOINTED A DELEGATE TO THE PARIS PEACE CONFERENCE.

IF THIS NOBLE AND GRAND IDEA FAILS, THE NEXT WAR WILL BE INFINITELY MORE TERRIBLE... BUT EVERYONE TURNS MY IDEAS DOWN...THEY THINK OF ME AS A MERE SCIENTIST!

IN 1905 MARCONI HAD MARRIED THE HON. BEATRICE O'BRIEN.

OH BEA!

DARLING!

BUT AFTER THE WAR...

WHERE'S DADDY?

HE MUST BE ON HIS YACHT, DEGNA.

MARCONI WAS MUCH SOUGHT AFTER IN THE WORLD OF HIGH SOCIETY. HE SPENT A LOT OF TIME ON HIS YACHT, ELETTRA, ENTERTAINING FRIENDS...

...SOME OF THEM VERY IMPORTANT.

YOU CONQUEROR OF THE SPACES, I NEED YOUR ADVICE AND SUPPORT.

I WOULD BE HONOURED, IL **DUCE**.

IN 1926, MUSSOLINI, NOW DICTATOR OF ITALY, CONGRATULATED MARCONI ON THE SUCCESS OF THE NEW IMPERIAL WIRELESS SCHEME, OR BEAM SYSTEM, BASED ON SHORT WAVE SIGNALS TRANSMITTED IN A NARROW BEAM ('**FASCIO**' IN ITALIAN — LITERALLY 'A BUNDLE OF STICKS').

LATER, DESCRIBING HIS '**SISTEME ONDE CORTE A FASCIO**'...

HA HA!

I WAS THE FIRST **FASCIST** IN ITALY!

WELL SAID!

MARCONI HAD, IN FACT, JOINED THE ITALIAN FASCIST PARTY IN 1923.

THROUGHOUT THE NEXT DECADE, MARCONI **CONTINUED** TO EXPERIMENT WITH SHORT-WAVES.

MUCH OF HIS WORK WAS CARRIED OUT ON THE **ELETTRA**, WHICH HE USED AS A MOBILE LABORATORY.

AFTER HIS DIVORCE FROM BEATRICE IN 1924, MARCONI MARRIED CRISTINA BEZZI-SCALI IN 1927.

CHEESE!!

BEZZI-SCALI'S FATHER WAS A HIGHLY PLACED OFFICIAL IN, AND NOBLEMAN OF, THE **VATICAN**, WHERE, IN 1931, MARCONI INSTALLED A SHORT-WAVE RADIO STATION.

THIS GAVE THE POPE A MEANS OF COMMUNICATION INDEPENDENT OF THE ITALIAN GOVERNMENT.

FASCIST PROPAGANDA IS TRYING TO DIRECT THE SPIRIT OF ITALIAN YOUTH TOWARDS THE EXCLUSIVE DEVOTION OF THE STATE! **OURS** MUST DIRECT IT **BACK TO GOD**!

BY THE 1930's, MARCONI HAD BEGUN TO BE INTERESTED IN VERY NARROW BEAMS, **MICRO-WAVES** AS WE CALL THEM TODAY.

NOW HE ARRANGED FOR A MICROWAVE LINK TO CONNECT POPE PIUS XI'S SUMMER RESIDENCE WITH THE CITY.

THIS WILL GIVE YOU **INSTANT** AND **PRIVATE** TELEPHONE CONTACT WITH YOUR STAFF.

WORK WITH MICROWAVES CONFIRMED WHAT HE HAD NOTICED BEFORE WITH SHORT-WAVES...

IF AN OBJECT PASSES **THROUGH** THE BEAM OF MICROWAVES, IT MAKES A HISSING NOISE IN THE RECEIVER!

BY 1935, HE WAS ABLE TO DEMONSTRATE THE PRINCIPLES OF WHAT CAME TO BE CALLED **RADAR**...

WHEN A BEAM OF MICROWAVES HITS A DISTANT OBJECT, ITS DIRECTION CAN BE LOCATED AND ITS DISTANCE MEASURED BY THE TIME TAKEN FOR THE RADIO WAVES TO RETURN TO THE RECEIVING AERIAL.

MY DISCOVERY CAN BE USED FOR THE SAFE PASSAGE OF SHIPS AND AIRCRAFT!

BUT HIS IDEA WAS SUPERSEDED BY MILITARY DEMANDS. SOON, ALL THE WORK WAS CLASSIFIED SECRET AND U.K. NATIONALS AT THE ITALIAN MARCONI CO. WERE SACKED AND REPLACED BY ITALIANS.

WHETHER OR NOT THE ENGLISH MARCONI CO. KNEW OF THE WORK OF ITS ITALIAN COUNTERPART, RADAR STATIONS WERE SET UP IN THE U.K. FROM 1937.

THE COMPANY LATER DEVELOPED THE RADAR (AND RADAR JAMMING) EQUIPMENT THAT HELPED TO CHANGE THE COURSE OF THE SECOND WORLD WAR.

IN 1935 MARCONI UNDERTOOK DIPLOMATIC MISSIONS ABROAD, TRYING TO REPAIR THE DAMAGE DONE TO ITALY'S INTERNATIONAL REPUTATION BY ITS **UN-DECLARED** WAR WITH ABYSSINIA.

DON'T GO TO BRAZIL, FATHER! YOU HAVE HAD HEART ATTACKS— YOUR HEALTH WILL SUFFER!

MUSSOLINI MAY NOT HEED MY ADVICE, DEGNA, BUT **ITALY** NEEDS MY HELP! I AM AN ITALIAN FIRST!

ITALY HAD A LOT TO ANSWER FOR: DETERMINED TO AVENGE HER EARLIER DEFEAT IN ERITREA, **IL DUCE** WAS USING AIR AND TANK POWER AND POISON GAS TO ANNEXE ABYSSINIA. HAILE SELASSIE WAS DEPOSED AND KING VICTOR EMMANUEL OF ITALY DECLARED KING.

IN ENGLAND, MARCONI APPROACHED JOHN **REITH**, DIRECTOR-GENERAL OF THE **BBC**...

IF ONLY THE COUNTRY OF MY **ADOPTION** WOULD UNDERSTAND THE ACTIONS OF THE COUNTRY OF MY **BIRTH**!

LET ME BROADCAST A FAIR AND UN-BIASSED ACCOUNT OF THE ABYSSINIAN CAMPAIGN.

HAS MUSSOLINI PUT YOU UP TO THIS? ...HE DOES NOT DENY IT! A CLEVER MOVE!

THE BBC REFUSED THE REQUEST OF THE MAN WHO HAD MADE BROADCASTING POSSIBLE. HE RETURNED TO ITALY AND CONTINUED HIS WORK ON MICROWAVES UNTIL HIS DEATH IN 1937. THE NEXT DAY, RADIO STATIONS ALL OVER THE WORLD OBSERVED A TWO-MINUTE SILENCE IN HIS HONOUR. *THE END*

Chapter 2

BROADCASTING BEGINS

MARCONI himself had been more interested in the use of his discovery for point to point communication than for reaching a wide number of people.

The sisters Levey in their Ostrich Dance. Photograph from *The Sketch*, August 22, 1894.

Music halls and *popular theatres* flourished, *sport* was increasingly organised as a spectator entertainment (e.g. the F.A. Cup dates from 1872; the first Olympic Games of modern times were held in 1896) and – with education-for-all and growing literacy – the *circulating library*, the *magazine* and the *popular newspaper* could count on an increasing readership.

Lord Northcliffe launches the *Daily Mail*, 1896.

'*Photographed reality*' began to appear in newspapers. With **George Eastman's** mass production of the Kodak from 1888 and the arrival of the snapshot, the camera became the prized possession of 'ordinary people'.

The *cinematograph* took little over a decade after its emergence in the 1890s to change from the nickelodeon in the fairground to an organised industry, and for cinema-going to become a firmly established social habit.

The Lumière brothers shrewdly anticipated the success of their invention. By its launch in 1896, they had built up a stock of machines and camera operators to shoot and project their films worldwide.

The *phonograph* made possible the growth of a music industry – and musical tastes to match.

Most of the new mass-produced machines had to be fed – a camera needs film, a phonograph needs records. But beyond the machine (or hardware) and its food (or software) a whole infrastructure of production, packing and distribution was necessary. Today, these separate functions are undertaken by different industries; but in the early years, as we have seen with the Lumière brothers, the inventors of the hardware also had to produce the software and market it themselves.

There's a chicken-and-egg problem for the inventors here. Who wants something before it's invented? How can the price of hardware and software be brought down sufficiently to ensure volume sales?

The mass production of cameras and phonographs (and washing machines, refrigerators and motor cars) was promoted by the development of new mass advertising techniques. Advertising 'creates' and sustains demand through the launch of the new device and its associated software.

This was the social climate, the network of interrelated products, habits and tastes, that greeted the first 'broadcasts'.

WE'VE seen how the state and armed forces eagerly seized on Marconi's invention to help them send messages from point to point without wires. What wasn't appreciated at the time was the possibility for *mass* entertainment which arose from the finding that wireless waves normally spread in all directions. (In fact this was seen as a positive drawback!)

It's not surprising that it was in the USA, where the emergence of a 'mass audience' was most advanced, that the domestic use of wireless telephony was first suggested.

THE FIRST USE OF THE WORD 'BROADCASTING' TO DESCRIBE TRANSMITTING BY WIRELESS TELEGRAPHY WAS IN THE UNITED STATES. ORIGINALLY IT MEANT TO SCATTER OR SOW SEED OVER A WIDE AREA.

B-BUT THAT MEANS EVERY-ONE CAN HEAR IT !!

In 1906, **Lee De Forest** had patented the crucially important triode valve, or **amplifier**, which was to make the reception of faint signals more effective and pave the way for *voice transmission*. On Christmas Eve the same year, **Reginald Fessenden**'s voice broadcasts from his station on the coast of Massachusetts had astonished ships' wireless operators over a wide area and a range of hundreds of miles.

THEY HEARD ME READING A PASSAGE FROM THE BIBLE...

...AND THE VIOLIN PLAYING!

...AND A WOMAN SINGING...

The Life and Work of **Lee De Forest**

Working for Western Electric, De Forest began to broadcast phonograph records and live singing from his New York laboratory and, in 1908, from the Eiffel Tower in Paris. By 1916 he was making frequent broadcasts – including a speech by his mother-in-law demanding votes for women, and the 1916 Presidential election results.

At American Marconi, **David Sarnoff** (famous for his reception of the Titanic SOS signals) wrote in 1916:

'*I HAVE IN MIND A PLAN OF DEVELOPMENT WHICH WOULD MAKE RADIO A HOUSEHOLD UTILITY. THE IDEA IS TO BRING MUSIC INTO THE HOUSE BY WIRELESS.*

'*A RADIO TELEPHONE TRANSMITTER HAVING A RANGE OF SAY 25 TO 30 MILES CAN BE INSTALLED AT A FIXED POINT WHERE INSTRUMENTAL OR VOCAL MUSIC... ARE PRODUCED... THE RECEIVER CAN BE DESIGNED IN THE FORM OF A SIMPLE RADIO MUSIC BOX AND ARRANGED FOR SEVERAL DIFFERENT WAVELENGTHS WHICH WOULD BE CHANGEABLE WITH THE THROWING OF A SWITCH OR PRESSING OF A BUTTON'.*'

YOU BUY 'EM UP! (SEE P. 59)

It was a good idea, inspired no doubt by the boom in sales of phonograph records (itself spurring on the craze for popular – especially jazz – music). But in spite of De Forest's increasingly successful voice transmissions, the Marconi Co. rejected Sarnoff's idea.

The EXPERIMENTER

A period of widespread experimentation followed. The big firms battled over patents to keep for themselves the expanding field of research and profitable development, though lone scientists and amateurs continued to make important discoveries.

U.S. PATENTS

SEND FOR THIS FORM

Don't Lose Your Rights

Invention Now Taught

Great Inventors Now Show You How to Make Your Ideas Pay

[55]

As USUAL, **war** was the catalyst for further developments.

When the First World War came to an end in 1918, practical broadcasting came about in the leading industrialised counties thanks to three kinds of pressure.

The first came from the **manufacturers**. Deprived of sales to the military, they needed a market for their radio components.

Hmm.... I suppose there's no chance of converting these **radio valves** into light bulbs....

Well, General, if **you** don't need 'em, there are some fellas out there who might give us a buck or two...

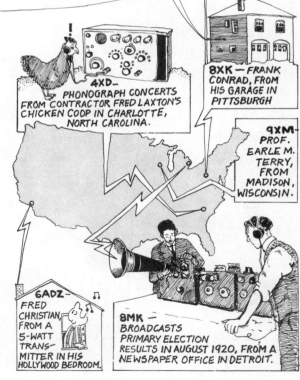

The second pressure came from the **amateurs**, most of them ex-servicemen who had learned to build and operate wirelesses in the forces.

In the USA, amateurs using first-class, up-to-date ex-military equipment numbered 125,000.

But the third pressure came from the **state**; and for that, back to the UK.

4XD— PHONOGRAPH CONCERTS FROM CONTRACTOR FRED LAXTON'S CHICKEN COOP IN CHARLOTTE, NORTH CAROLINA.

8XK — FRANK CONRAD, FROM HIS GARAGE IN PITTSBURGH

9XM— PROF. EARLE M. TERRY, FROM MADISON, WISCONSIN.

6ADZ— FRED CHRISTIAN, FROM A 5-WATT TRANSMITTER IN HIS HOLLYWOOD BEDROOM.

8MK — BROADCASTS PRIMARY ELECTION RESULTS IN AUGUST 1920, FROM A NEWSPAPER OFFICE IN DETROIT.

The British government, accustomed through the war years to a policy of secrecy and control, feared political instability.

An event in Dublin in 1916 had signalled to the British the need for the greatest security. Rebels had seized the central Post Office and from a ship's transmitter in the Institute of Telegraphy had broadcast morse-code bulletins bringing uncensored reports of the **Easter Rising** to the outside world.

"T.H.E... B.R.I.T.I.S.H.
... T.R.O.O.P.S ...
H.A.V.E ... B.E.E.N ...
F.I.R.I.N.G ... O.N ...
O.U.R ... W.O.M.E.N ..."

More earth-shaking still was the **Bolshevik Revolution** of 1917 with its proclaimed aim of spreading world revolution by every means available.

WE WERE ONLY THE SPARK: THE FLAMES WERE SPREADING!

ТОВ. Ленин ОЧИЩАЕТ ЗЕМЛЮ ОТ НЕЧИСТИ.

During a short-lived revolution in Germany in 1919, the **Soldiers' and Workers' Council** took over the military wireless network and used it to broadcast 'To All' the aims and progress of the revolution. This 'Bolshevism in the German radio system' terrified the British authorities.

IF TRANSMISSION IS ALLOWED TO **EVERYONE** ... THE **BOLSHEVIST** ELEMENT WOULD VERY SOON MAKE FULL USE OF THE OPPORTUNITIES ... TO THE **DETRIMENT** OF THE COUNTRY!!

These three pressures worked in different ways on each side of the Atlantic.

In the USA, a Bill backed by the US Navy and designed to give the government complete control of broadcasting was defeated. Instead, a commercial monopoly was created. In 1919, General Electric, Westinghouse, AT&T and United Fruit joined forces to create the **Radio Corporation of America**. RCA soon bought out American Marconi to gain access to its patent pool of more than 2000 key electronic inventions.

So in the USA the manufacturers won.

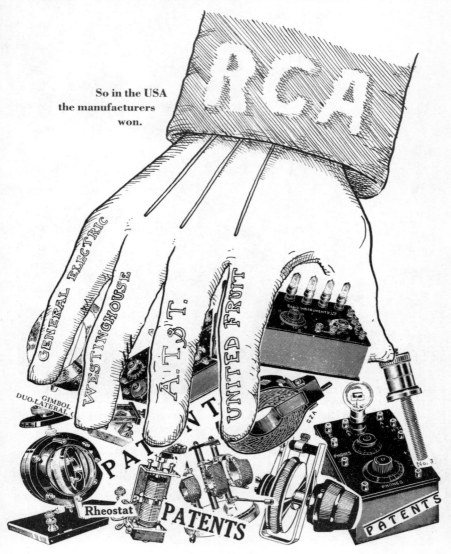

The Broadcasters

KDKA was the first station owned by a company, Westinghouse. On November 2, 1920, it broadcast the Presidential Election results and phonograph music over a four hour period.

This was the start of **wireless fever**. Hundreds of stations began to go on air.

At first the idea was that the money was to be made from the sale of receiving sets, or simply by a 'toll' payment for use of airtime.

'We were to provide no programmes. The public was to come in. Anyone who had a message for the world or wished to entertain was to come in and pay their money as they would upon coming into a telephone booth, address the world and go out'. (AT&T)

From this it was a short step to the **first advertisement**. In 1927, an executive of the Queensboro Corporation promoted the sale of apartments in Jackson Heights, on Long Island.

LET ME ENJOIN YOU AS YOU VALUE YOUR HEALTH AND YOUR HOPES AND YOUR HOME HAPPINESS, GET AWAY FROM THE SOLID MASSES OF BRICK ... WHERE CHILDREN GROW UP STARVED FOR A RUN OVER A PATCH OF GRASS AND THE SIGHT OF A TREE ..

The same year, more than 500 stations went on air in the U.S.

Time for us big guys to move in and make a network outa this chickenfeed!

By 1927 the pattern of American broadcasting had been established. Three networks had been formed – CBS and the Red and Blue networks of NBC – and Congress had passed the Radio Act (1927) which set up the **Federal Radio Commission** (later the Federal Communications Commission).

THE ETHER WILL BE FILLED WITH **FRANTIC CHAOS** ... FOR THE FIRST TIME AN INDUSTRY IS **BEGGING** TO BE **REGULATED!**

   Herbert Hoover, then Secretary of Commerce, was responsible. Central control was necessary or...

PALMOLIVE RADIO HOUR—Broadcast every Wednesday nights from 9:30 to 10:30 p.m. eastern time; 8:30 to 9:30 p.m. central time; 7:30 to 8:30 p.m. mountain time; 6:30 to 7:30 p.m. Pacific Coast time over station WEAF and 37 stations associated with The National Broadcasting Company.

"Hit of the Air"—Williams Radio Hours
"Hit of the Air": Williams Sync-O-Matics—Tune in Two Nights Each Week. Williams Sync-O-Matics—Tune in Tuesday on Station WJZ and Associated NBC Stations at 10 o'clock Eastern Standard Time. Williams Mel-O-Matics—Tune in Friday on WGN, Chicago, 8:30 Central Standard Time.

According to one US critic of the system, writing in *Our Master's Voice* (1936):

"THE AMERICAN APPARATUS OF **AD-VERTISING** IS SOME-THING UNIQUE IN HISTORY ... IT IS LIKE A **GROTESQUE, SMIRKING, GARGOYLE** SET AT THE VERY TOP OF AMERICA'S SKY-SCRAPING ADVENTURE IN **ACQUISITION AD INFINITUM** ...THE GARGOYLE'S MOUTH IS A **LOUDSPEAKER**, POWERED BY THE VESTED INTERESTS OF A **TWO-BILLION DOLLAR INDUSTRY**, AND BACK OF THAT THE VESTED INTERESTS OF **BUSINESS** AS A WHOLE, OF **INDUSTRY**, OF **FINANCE**".

JAMES RORTY

Back in the UK, the Marconi Company broadcast daily programmes from Chelmsford in the spring of 1920. On 15 June, at the suggestion of Lord Northcliffe of the *Daily Mail*, Dame Nellie Melba gave a broadcast which fired people's imagination all over Europe. She began with a long silvery trill ('my hello to the world'), sang in English, Italian and French and ended with 'God Save the King'. But by the autumn complaints were growing from the military about this 'frivolous' use of a national service...

As *The Financier* reported in August 1920:

'A few days ago the pilot of a Vickers Vimy machine was crossing the Channel in a thick fog and was trying to obtain weather and landing reports from Lympne. All he could hear was a musical evening.'

'THE QUESTION MAY WELL BE ASKED WHY WAS IT THAT **WIRELESS TELEPHONY** DID NOT COME INTO GENERAL USE IN THE AUTUMN OF 1920, WHEN THINGS WERE JUST BEGINNING TO BOOM IN AMERICA? THE ANSWER LIES IN A SENTENCE: **"WE ARE BRITISH"**. LET **OTHERS** RUSH AT THE NEW INVENTIONS, AND DO THE EXPERIMENTING, SPEND THE MONEY, GET THE **HARD KNOCKS** ... **WE BRITISH SIT TIGHT AND LOOK BEFORE WE LEAP.'**

C A Lewis (Organiser of BBC Programmes), *Broadcasting From Within*, 1924.

The truth was that the state wanted to keep the technology to itself: the **Imperial Communications Committee** enforced a two year moratorium on broadcasting.

So, though amateurs could receive concerts from the Hague and Paris there was silence on the airwaves in Britain. A petition from 63 Wireless Societies was handed in to the Post Office in December 1921.

As a concession, the **Marconi Company** were allowed to broadcast half an hour a week. The Post Office insisted that there was a break every three minutes for the operator to listen out for official messages.

The first such broadcast was made (by **Peter Eckersley**, later the BBC's Chief Engineer) on February 14, 1922, from an ex-army hut at Writtle, near Chelmsford.

In May 1922, Marconi's **2LO** was allowed to broadcast from the Company's headquarters in the Strand.

Other companies were also willing and able to broadcast, and – more profitable as they saw it – to manufacture wireless receivers. One hundred applications for licences were received by the Post Office.

The solution adopted by the Government was to persuade the companies to form a consortium – the **British Broadcasting Company**. At the time the official reason was that only a few frequencies were available to be shared out. But the Government could have organised things differently. It depends on which way you want to cut the cake: many small low-powered stations or a few high-powered ones.

Warned by the capitalist anarchy of US free enterprise on one side and the awful spectre of Bolshevik Russia on the other, a decentralised solution did not appeal to the British.

It certainly made sense from a security point of view that central government should maintain overall control of broadcasting – but it would do so from a distance.

Broadcasting was to be treated as a public utility – like gas, water, or the Post Office – and after two official inquiries the shape of the new public service was set. Licensed by Royal Charter and presided over by a board appointed by the government as 'trustees of the national interest', the renamed **British Broadcasting Corporation** would be financed by a licence fee paid by each owner of a wireless set. This gave the BBC an assured and increasing audience, with relative independence from direct government control.

A crucial figure promoting this comfortable relationship with government was the Managing Director of the Company, later the Director-General of the Corporation, **John Reith**. Described by A.J.P. Taylor as 'Calvinist in upbringing, harsh and ruthless in character', Reith passed an important test even before the Corporation officially started.

With all the newspapers (except the Government's *British Gazette*) closed down, **Winston Churchill** (the Home Secretary) wanted to commandeer the BBC, but Reith argued that if he did so the crisis would be exacerbated...

The **General Strike** gave the BBC a national audience and set the pattern for its relations with government.

IN THE EARLY YEARS the local BBC stations enjoyed considerable independence. Under the pressure of Reith's policy of centralised control, however, local radio as such gradually disappeared and was replaced by a National and a Regional Service. Despite (or perhaps because of) Reith's use of the Regions as a place of banishment for troublesome producers, much good work was produced there; work which tried genuinely to reflect working class concerns in a decade when unemployment and poverty were widespread.

North Region was particularly strong in talent. **E.A. Harding** recruited a group of writers and performers, including **Joan Littlewood** and **Ewan McColl**.

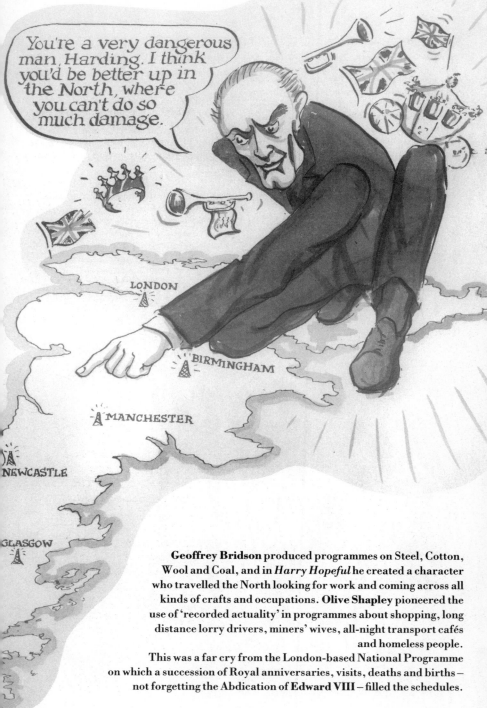

Geoffrey **Bridson** produced programmes on Steel, Cotton, Wool and Coal, and in *Harry Hopeful* he created a character who travelled the North looking for work and coming across all kinds of crafts and occupations. Olive **Shapley** pioneered the use of 'recorded actuality' in programmes about shopping, long distance lorry drivers, miners' wives, all-night transport cafés and homeless people.

This was a far cry from the London-based National Programme on which a succession of Royal anniversaries, visits, deaths and births – not forgetting the Abdication of **Edward VIII** – filled the schedules.

[71]

As the BBC grew, Reith's conception of public service set the tone.

'Our responsibility is to carry into the greatest possible number of homes everything that is best in every human department of knowledge, endeavour and achievement, and to avoid the things which are, or may be hurtful... It is occasionally represented to us that we are apparently setting out to give the public what we think they need, and not what they want, but few know what they want, and very few what they need. There is often no difference... Better to overestimate the mentality of the public than to underestimate it.'

It was in this period that the traditions and conventions were laid down which were still typical of the BBC decades later. By its staff selection procedure and its policy of 'referral up', the BBC built a reputation for 'impartial' programming. Its staff were safe, and its Governors were wholly drawn from the list of 'the great and the good' (the 400 names kept by the Director of Public Appointments Unit of the Civil Service Department).

'The BBC. . . developed into a kind of domestic diplomatic service, representing the British to the British. BBC culture, like BBC standard English, was. . . an intellectual ambience composed out of the values, standards and beliefs of the professional middle class, especially that

part educated at Oxford and Cambridge. Sports, popular music and entertainment which appealed to the lower classes were included in large measure in the programmes, but the manner in which they were purveyed, the content and the presentation remained indomitably upper middle class,' Tom Burns, *The BBC – Public Institution and Private World* (1977).

'IMPARTIAL' IS THAT WHICH DOES NOT OFFEND ME AND MY FRIENDS ... OH ... ER ... AND, OF COURSE, THE HON. MEMBERS OPPOSITE!

Later generations of staff were drawn from a wider class range, but control remained in establishment hands. Given the BBC's class filter and its narrow definition of 'political' which marginalises or ignores any views outside the bounds of the Parliamentary consensus, we can see that, for the BBC, 'impartial' is a relative term.

When Reith left the BBC in 1938, one newspaper congratulated him for making the BBC as thoroughly typical and representative as the Bank of England.

REITH has been accused of 'using the brute force of the monopoly to stamp Christian morality on the British people.' Certainly his suffocating Sunday schedules drove listeners to **Radio Luxembourg** (and **Radio Normandie**) in their thousands. It was Britain's first encounter with American-style commercial radio, though US-based multinationals had already spread their tentacles throughout Latin America and the Far East.

Set up in 1934, Radio Luxembourg based its programming on a simple but successful formula: find out the programmes an audience is not being allowed to listen to, broadcast them from a station outside the jurisdiction of the country concerned and finance it all by advertising from agencies who otherwise have no broadcast outlet at home.

Hallo hallo
Pols-key rah-djo
Var~shah~va!

1926 IRELAND
1926 GUYANA
1927 INDIA
1927 KENYA
1931 THAILAND
1935 GHANA
1936 TUNISIA
1938 LEBANON
1939 NIGERIA
1941 ETHIOPIA
1942 JAMAICA
1945 CHINA
1948 CYPRUS
1949 SAUDI ARABIA
1951 TANZANIA
1959 TIBET

By the 1930s, many countries had started their own domestic services, and several were using radio both to influence foreign audiences and to reach their colonial 'subjects' around the world (the BBC's Empire Service was launched in 1932).

MEANWHILE the **directly political power of radio** was also being further advanced at home – **Roosevelt's** 'fireside chats' were thought to be a cohesive force in the dark days of the Depression, and **Mussolini's** voice could be heard in the remotest Italian villages.

The **Nazis** attached great importance to radio propaganda, and **Hitler's** speeches became a familiar sound in Europe – and even further afield thanks to high-powered and well-financed short-wave broadcasts.

During the Spanish Civil War, a huge radio transmitter supplied by the Germans enabled the voice of the Nationalists to be heard throughout Spain. At 10pm each night Republicans and Nationalists alike were enthralled by the outrageous broadcasts of **General Queipo de Llano**. When **Franco** excluded him from his cabinet de Llano retaliated by stopping the broadcasts.

On September 3, 1939, Germany invaded Poland. Chamberlain sent Hitler an ultimatum to withdraw...

*....I have to tell you that no such undertaking has been received and consequently **Britain is at war with Germany.***

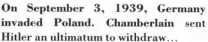

*This is **Jairmany** calling, **Jairmany** calling...*

During the 'phoney war' period (1939-40), with the popular foreign commercial stations (Luxembourg, Normandie) closed down and the BBC confining itself to repeated news bulletins and serious music, British audiences were entertained by William Joyce – **Lord Haw-Haw** – a propagandist working for the Germans. By the end of 1939, 30% of the population listened to him regularly.

Meanwhile bored troops in the barrack rooms demanded more entertainment from the BBC – so the *Forces Programme* was born, a deliberate concession to popular taste.

*(SIGH!) Give us **Gracie Fields, Vera Lynn, Winston Churchill, Sandy Macpherson** on the theatre organ...*

Before long, boredom was forgotten.

June/July 1940: Dunkirk, the fall of France, the Battle of Britain.

Once again, war interrupted worldwide communications, yet its effect on radio was stimulating. Audiences increased dramatically and so did the budgets for research and development.

With all of Europe under Nazi occupation, the BBC's Foreign Services were the only source of news from the Allies' point of view. Listened to in secret, and despite Nazi jamming and penalties for being caught, the BBC's wartime broadcasts helped sustain morale in mainland Europe. They could also be used to carry coded messages for Resistance fighters.

General de Gaulle broadcasting to the Fighting French Forces in 1941.

"CALLING ALL FORCES OVERSEAS...

AT HOME, programmes broadcast from factory's lunch hours *(Workers' Playtime, Music While You Work)* were interspersed with news that didn't pull punches. (Though for a long time the BBC went along with Churchill's virtual ban on any open discussion of 'post-war reconstruction'.) Variety and comedy shows tried to reflect rather than direct the language and attitudes of working people and members of the armed forces. After 1942, when US troops began to be stationed in Britain in large numbers, shows became more Americanised.

Women welders broadcasting on the BBC's *Bridgebuilders*.

– DON'T MIND IF I DO..!
– CAN I DO YOU NOW, SIR?
– THIS IS FUNF SPEAKING....
– GEE, BOSS! SUMP'N' TERRIBLE'S HAPPENED!
– DON'T FORGET THE DIVER!

IT'S THAT MAN AGAIN

TA TA FOR NOW!

"THIS IS LONDON....

"THERE ARE NO WORDS TO DESCRIBE THE THING THAT IS HAPPENING"

.... AND **THE RAID** WHICH STARTED ABOUT SEVEN HOURS AGO IS **STILL IN PROGRESS**..."

"LET ME TELL YOU WHAT'S HAPPENED IN THE **WARSAW GHETTO**. IT WAS NEVER A PLEASANT PLACE EVEN IN PEACETIME...

"WHAT IS HAPPENING IS **THIS**: MILLIONS OF HUMAN BEINGS, MOST OF THEM JEWS, ARE BEING GATHERED UP WITH RUTHLESS EFFICIENCY AND MURDERED...

" A WOMAN STOOD ON THE CORNER, CLUTCHING A RATHER DIRTY PILLOW. A POLICEMAN WAS TRYING TO COMFORT HER. AND A FIREMAN SAID, `YOU'D BE SURPRISED WHAT STRANGE THINGS PEOPLE PICK UP WHEN THEY RUN OUT OF A BURNING HOUSE'...."

During the Blitz, **Ed Murrow's** vivid yet matter-of-fact broadcasts from London for CBS gained him a national reputation back home — and swelled his network's ratings.

BLESS THEM ALL...

US radio was enormously boosted by the war. As the tide turned and troops were found in many remote places round the world, the *American Forces Radio Service* expanded. By the end of the war in 1945 it had 800 stations serving the troops overseas. These stations made liberated populations so familiar with pop music, commercials and the American way of life that audiences came to demand the same from their own broadcasters.

...a friendly American custom lan...

In Flemish, it's *vriendelijkheid*. In American it's the plain, everyday word *friendliness*. And everywhere your Yankee doughboy goes, it comes spontaneously from his heart in a good old home-town phrase, *Have a Coke*. That's the way he's letting our democratic allies know what he does the friendly things he does. Friendliness is bred in his bone, and to kindred spirit it bubbles out—like the bubbling goodness of Coca-Cola itself and everything American that's behind it. Yes, the pause that refreshes with ice-cold Coke becomes an ambassador of good... the old home spirit carried across the seas.

Our fighting men meet up... on the spot. Coca-Cola ha...

It's hardly surprising, then, that television, an infant technology at the time of the Second World War, was to be shaped by the same forces as had created radio.

Chapter 3   TALES FROM

TELEVISION

TELEVISION had been
an experimental
possibility for as long as
radio, with the same
uncoordinated scattering
of research across the
international scientific
community.

In 1884 the German **Paul Nipkow** patented a rotating disc through whose apertures an image was scanned. *Mechanical scanning* was the basis for much subsequent work, including **John Logie Baird's** in Britain, though it eventually proved to be a cul-de-sac.

In 1897, **Ferdinand Braun** invented the *cathode ray tube*, a glass vessel containing an electrode which, when heated, emitted electrons in a beam or ray.

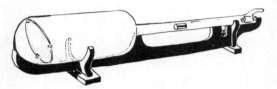

By focussing the beam on fluorescent paint at the end of the tube, Braun found he could produce a bright spot of light. The spot could be made to move about if he deflected the beam with electro-magnets.

In 1913, **Elster** and **Geitel** developed a *photo-electric cell* which generated electrical pulses when exposed to light, the strength of the pulse varying in strength according to the amount of light falling upon the cell.

In the USA in 1917, **Moore** patented a *neon gas discharge lamp* whose brightness depended on the strength of the electric pulses it received.

The Inventors

A trio of gifted Russians working at the University of St Petersburg also had a far-reaching influence.

U.S.S.R

St. Petersburg

NGLAND

GERMANY

In 1907 **Boris Rosing** designed a *cathode ray receiver*. A photo-electric cell converted the light passing through the holes of Nipkow's disc into electric signals. These signals were received by a cathode ray tube whose beam was made to move up and down the light sensitive screen at the end of the tube in a fraction of a second, thereby creating crude images.

The amateur experimenter and scientist **A.A. Campbell-Swinton** wrote about a system of 'distant electric vision' in *Nature* as early as 1908. A further paper in 1911 proposed using cathode ray beams to scan both 'required surfaces' – scene and screen. This accurate basic proposal makes Campbell-Swinton the true inventor of the modern TV system.

Isaac Schoenberg came to Britain in 1915 and eventually became head of the EMI team which invented the successful *electronic scanning screen* adopted by the BBC.

After emigrating to the USA **Vladimir Zworykin** worked on similar lines as Schoenberg for Westinghouse and then RCA. His discoveries effectively created American television.

TELEVISION

BASICALLY, WHAT IS GOING ON IN THE MAKING OF TV PICTURES IS THE 'SCANNING' OF A SCENE BY A CAMERA, MUCH AS YOUR EYE IS SCANNING THE LINES OF PRINT ON THIS PAGE.

1. SCENE

2. LIGHT FROM SCENE

3. LENS
FOCUSES LIGHT ONTO MIRRORS

4. MIRRORS
SPLIT THE LIGHT INTO RED, GREEN AND BLUE.

5. ELECTRON 'GUNS'
IN EACH CAMERA TUBE 'FIRE' A STREAM OF ELECTRONS AT THE LIGHT WHICH IS REGISTERED BY A SCREEN OF PHOTO-ELECTRIC CELLS. THESE LIGHT-SENSITIVE CELLS 'READ' THE PATTERN OF LIGHT AND DARK AND CONVERT IT INTO ELECTRICAL IMPULSES.

6. ELECTRICAL IMPULSES
ARE ENCODED INTO SEPARATE 'BLACK AND WHITE' AND COLOUR SIGNALS WHICH ARE THEN COMBINED AS ONE COMPLETE SIGNAL TO BE TRANSMITTED.

7. TRANSMISSION
IS ACHIEVED IN EXACTLY THE SAME WAY AS RADIO, BUT TV TAKES UP MORE FREQUENCY SPACE, AS EXPLAINED ON PAGE 31.

8. TELEVISION RECEIVER
DECODES THE SIGNAL INTO SEPARATE COLOUR SIGNALS WHICH ARE FED INTO THREE ELECTRON GUNS.

9. ELECTRONS
ARE 'FIRED' BY THE 'GUNS' ALONG LINES OF PHOSPHOR DOTS ON THE TV SCREEN. THE STRENGTH OF THE ELECTRICAL IMPULSES REFLECTS THE PATTERN OF LIGHT.

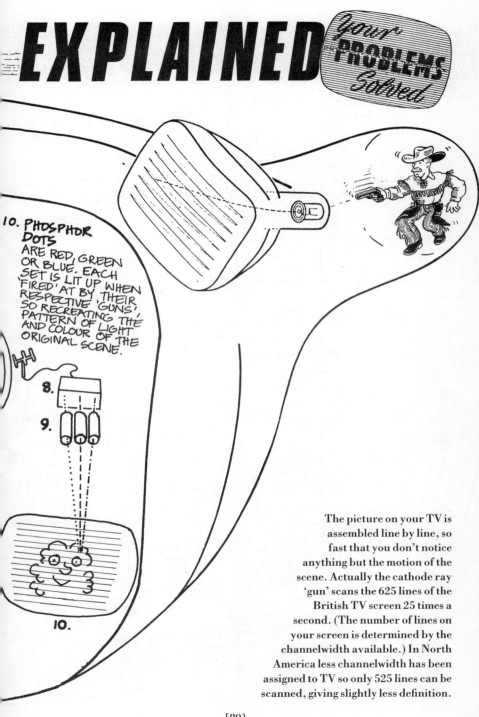

10. PHOSPHOR DOTS ARE RED, GREEN OR BLUE. EACH SET IS LIT UP WHEN 'FIRED' AT BY THEIR RESPECTIVE 'GUNS', SO RECREATING THE PATTERN OF LIGHT AND COLOUR OF THE ORIGINAL SCENE.

8.

9.

10.

The picture on your TV is assembled line by line, so fast that you don't notice anything but the motion of the scene. Actually the cathode ray 'gun' scans the 625 lines of the British TV screen 25 times a second. (The number of lines on your screen is determined by the channelwidth available.) In North America less channelwidth has been assigned to TV so only 525 lines can be scanned, giving slightly less definition.

Nipkow's disc, which John Logie Baird developed, could at best only scan a 240-line screen. The disc spun rapidly between the subject being viewed and a photo-electric cell. As the disc spun, each hole in the disc revealed light from a different part of the subject, the whole of the object being covered by one revolution of the disc.

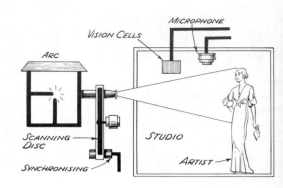

When the BBC started regular TV transmissions in 1936, they alternated between using Baird's system one week and the EMI-Marconi electronic system the next. The difference was marked. Baird's scanning system couldn't compete with the cathode ray gun, and the mobile Emitron camera was greatly superior to Baird's fixed and heavy machinery. **The EMI-Marconi system won the trial.**

Even so, it has been suggested that the main reason why the British government gave the go-ahead for the BBC to develop the Marconi-EMI system of television as early as 1936 was to provide a cover for Marconi UK to build the Chain Home Radar system (radar and television use the same valves).

Got to keep this **RADAR** stuff under wraps, chaps!

TELEVISION developed in several countries before the war. Germany started a regular filmed television service in 1935, using low-definition pictures. The idea was to install TV sets in public places or to project television pictures on large cinema screens using the equipment shown below. Although German TV's aim was to carry Nazi propaganda into the hearts and minds of viewers, the image of Aryan superiority was not improved by the broadcast of pictures of the black American Jesse Owens winning 4 gold medals at the 1936 Berlin Olympics (centre). The intermediate film transmitter van shown top was used for outside TV broadcasts.

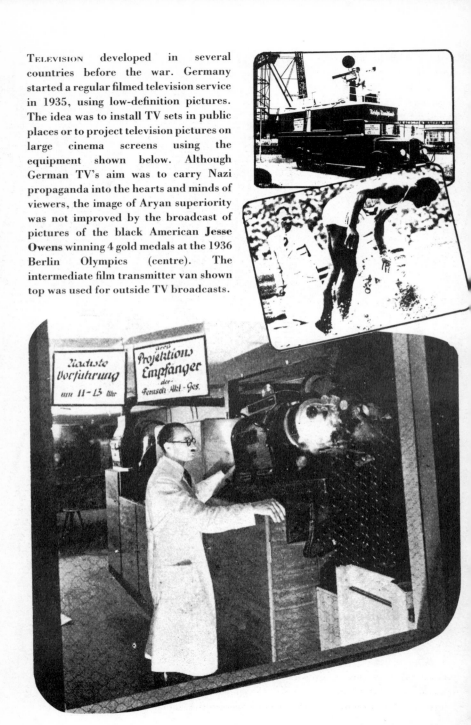

The BBC launched the world's first regular public service of high definition television in 1936. A Coronation (**George VI's**) came in handy for boosting sales of sets. The television pictures received by the HMV set in the advertisement (right) were viewed in an inclined mirror because the cathode ray tube was mounted in a vertical position.

World War Two arrived and the service closed down 'for the duration' with a Mickey Mouse film. Here Mickey is viewed directly on a Baird receiver of 1935.

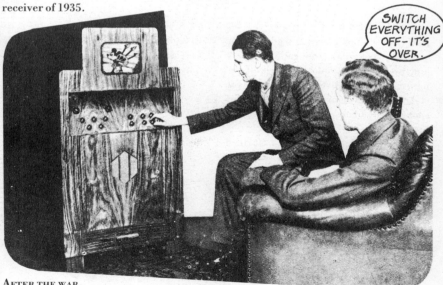

AFTER THE WAR,
British viewers were re-introduced to the genteel, night-out-in-the-West-End-tie-and-tails-type of television as if there'd never been an interruption. Announcers wore evening dress as they had done on radio.

It was in the USA that TV really got going, financed by the considerable profits from radio. (The radio networks' links with the music industry were being spurred on by competition. Columbia's LPs battled against RCA's 45s for air play by DJs invented by the newly created network ABC.)

But soon it was TV where the big profits were to be made, and advertising was attracted away from radio. Variety and 'sit-coms' became the staple of the new medium. Advertisers could pay for complete prográmmes, so it was easy for sponsors to bring pressure directly on programmes.

For example, you couldn't 'ford' a river in a Western sponsored by Chevrolet. And Ford are reported to have deleted a shot of the New York skyline because it showed the Chrysler building. In 1953, Kipling's *The Light That Failed* had to be broadcast as *The Gathering Night* because Westinghouse, who make light bulbs, was a sponsor. When the American Gas Association sponsored *Judgement at Nuremburg* all references to gas chambers were eliminated from the account of the holocaust.

1952 was the year TV took over the Presidential Elections. Whereas **Adlai Stevenson** refused to be merchandised 'like a breakfast food'…

… **Dwight Eisenhower** had his campaign planned down to the last detail by an advertising agency and spent a day recording 50 spot ads, each of 20 seconds duration.

receiving illicit funds. His performance became famous as the 'Checkers Speech' because he disarmed viewers with a story about a black and white spaniel sent to him by a supporter.

Richard Nixon, running as Ike's Vice President, used TV to reply to charges of

Eisenhower and Nixon won by an overwhelming majority.

Under Eisenhower, US hostility to the Soviet Union took on a new intensity, with anti-communist purges led by Senator Joe McCarthy. *Red Channels* listed alleged communist sympathisers in the broadcasting industries. In 1954 CBS were dismayed when it was revealed that the star of their high-rating show *I Love Lucy* had registered with the Communist Party in 1936, but were relieved when she was officially cleared of 'un-American activities'. It was said that she had only joined to please her grandfather.

COMMERCIAL T.V.

RAPIDLY EXPANDING POST-WAR ECONOMIES WERE DRIVING HARD FOR NEW MARKETS AMONG THE **NEWLY AFFLUENT**. TV **ADVERTISEMENTS** PROMISED TO BE THE VEHICLE THAT COULD DELIVER THIS VAST MASS OF CONSUMERS INTO THE HANDS OF BUSINESS.

THE **LABOUR PARTY** AND **TRADE UNION** MOVEMENT INITIALLY OPPOSED COMMERCIAL TV...

> This proposed development is totally against the **British temperament**, the **British way of life**, and the best or even reasonably good **British traditions!**
>
> Herbert Morrison, Labour MP.

1954

Here's to **Independent Television!**

Independent my *rse!

IN THE MAIN OPPOSITION WAS EITHER IGNORED OR MOLLIFIED BY THE TERMS OF FOUNDATION OF **ITV** IN 1954. IT WAS A BRILLIANT **EUPHEMISM** —ONE THAT SUGGESTED **SEPARATION** FROM GOVERNMENT CONTROL, A **FREE** SERVICE (THERE WERE NO EXTRA LICENCE FEES) AND A HIGH DEGREE OF **RESPECTABILITY**. IT WAS **CONTROLLED**, HOWEVER, BY AN AUTHORITY COMPOSED **WHOLLY** OF GOVERNMENT **APPOINTEES!**

THE **I.T.A** (INDEPENDENT TELEVISION AUTHORITY — NOW KNOWN AS THE **I.B.A.** OR **I**NDEPENDENT **B**ROADCASTING AUTHORITY) —
● LAID DOWN THE RULES OF ADVERTISING AND PREVIEWED ALL THE SCRIPTS FOR ADS
● APPROVED THE PROGRAMME SCHEDULES
● OWNED THE TRANSMITTERS
● MET IN **SECRET SESSION** (THEY STILL DO!) TO APPOINT THE PROGRAMME CONTRACTORS OR FRANCHISE HOLDERS FOR EACH REGION. WHEREAS IN THE USA ADVERTISERS COULD SPONSOR WHOLE PROGRAMMES, IN THE UK ADVERTISING IS '**SPOT ADVERTISING**' — IT IS SOLD AS SECTIONS OF TIME BETWEEN PROGRAMMES OR IN 'NATURAL BREAKS' WITHIN THEM. COMPARED WITH USA TELEVISION THESE BREAKS ARE SHORTER (THEY ARE LIMITED TO SIX MINUTES PER HOUR), LESS FREQUENT AND LESS OBTRUSIVE.

Successful US programming set the pattern. While Westerns, such as *Bonanza* and *Cheyenne*, had to be imported, quiz shows could be home-grown, with less outrageously huge prizes than their US counterparts. The formula was completed with variety, sit-coms and soap operas…

Soap operas had their origin in America of the 1930s when soap companies sponsored cheaply made daytime drama serials. TV in the 1950s copied the format of ongoing family sagas. The popularity of some soap operas is so great that they have had continuous runs for decades.

Something home-grown was needed for the British audience – different in style, more leisurely and downbeat. *Coronation Street* was the outstanding success. By 1985, its 25th anniversary, almost all its 2400 programmes had been in the Top 20.

ITV also adopted one-off 'social realist' plays, then very successful in the US but later killed off by advertisers who preferred the safer and more predictable format of the series.

Former Canadian Broadcasting Corporation's head of drama **Sydney Newman** was appointed to run ABC's *Armchair Theatre*. His productions 'were going to be about the very people who owned TV sets – which is the working class'. **The BBC had seen nothing like it.**

Despite their attempted sabotage of ITV's launch – a dramatic episode of BBC's long-running radio series, *The Archers*, had Grace Archer burned to death in a stable fire trying to rescue the horses – the Corporation was forced to realise that its claim to the universal licence fee was in danger. It injected some much needed cash and life into the TV service. In some ways competition was good for the BBC. In the early 1960s under the dynamic leadership of **Sir Hugh Carleton Greene**, BBC's *Play for To-day* (for which Newman was poached from ABC), current affairs and satire shows shocked and stimulated viewers, winning back for the BBC an equal ratings share.

In the long run the two adversaries grew more and more alike, each in different ways dependent on the audience and fearful of government.

Ten years after it began, ITV had become entrenched as a national institution.

IN THE expanding economy of the 1950s and 1960s advertising revenue grew astronomically, and TV companies found they were bringing in vast profits.

Crisis and recession in the mid-1970s set limits to advertising revenue. Some TV companies diversified their interests into paperback publishing, motorway services, leisure and travel, commercial radio and other aspects of media and entertainment.

TV programmes, too, were becoming more expensive, challenged by an increasingly sophisticated and jaded audience. Companies continued to buy in programmes from abroad more cheaply than they could produce them at home.

In principle, there were strict limits established at the start of ITV to ensure that not too many foreign programmes – i.e. US-made – are imported in order that British culture, jobs and productions are protected and encouraged. A limit of 14% – the 'foreign quota' – is supposed to be observed.

Of course British programme makers exported their programmes too.

The exchange is neither symmetrical nor equitable though, and the 'foreign quota' is regularly waived. In practice, the amount of apparently US material seen on British screens today is higher because of co-productions and pre-transmission sales agreements. Both are devices to overcome the increasingly high cost of TV production.

Since the early 1970s a number of ITV companies – and the BBC – have developed relationships with foreign TV companies to co-produce series. Other British-produced programmes don't get off the ground until their sale is guaranteed in advance on American networks. Either way, this means more and more British programmes have to appeal to foreign audiences. The result is either a sort of mid-Atlantic 'cops and robbers' or historical costume dramas that confirm tourist brochure clichés about British life.

In 1969, public television started *Sesame Street*, an educational series for pre-school children, with an East Harlem setting, puppets (later known as the Muppets), and a multi-racial cast. Its apparatus of research, merchandising and hard-sell 'advisory teams' made this a high budget, brilliantly animated commercial for American values both at home and for export worldwide.

Translated into *Plazo Sesamo*, *Sesamestrasse* or *Bonjour Sesame*, such an advertisement was badly needed.

The USA in the 1960s had been swept with guilt, confusions and insecurities. The decade that started so brightly with **Kennedy's** inauguration and his promises to end poverty and to win the space race, continued with a near disastrous confrontation with Russia over Cuba, Kennedy's own assassination and (later) those of his brother **Bobby** and the Civil Rights campaigner **Martin Luther King**. President Johnson's declaration of 'war on poverty', especially among urban blacks, did nothing to prevent a rising tide of race riots, urban insurrections and student unrest which swept the US. The people were asserting their demand for civil rights, but they were also protesting about their government's increasing involvement with the war in Vietnam.

THE WORLD had suddenly become smaller since satellite transmission (see the next chapter) brought these events – often live – to screens in almost every country. American television news reporting from Vietnam, and live coverage of Congressional hearings on the war, were influential in building up public opposition (at home and abroad) – and this despite increasing use of the media by the White House.

After TV pictures showed U.S. marines setting fire to a Vietnamese village in 1965, Johnson phoned the CBS President: 'Frank, are you trying to fuck me?... Yesterday your boys shat on the American flag.'

In 1968, protesters outside the Democratic Convention in Chicago chanted 'The Whole World is Watching' while police beat them in front of the news cameras (below). But the protest was not confined to the USA...

'Je participe, tu participes, il participe, nous participons, vous participez, ils profitent' (wall slogan, May 1968)

Violent police action broke up an anti-war demonstration in Britain in 1968, a year of student uprisings throughout Europe – especially in France. De Gaulle's manipulation of broadcasting during the Paris riots and sacking of protesting staff at ORTF brought French radio and TV into public discredit. And in Czechoslovakia, in August, pictures secretly fed through Austria allowed the whole world to watch Soviet tanks crushing the Prague Spring (of 'socialism with a human face').

INTERNATIONAL sporting events, covered live on TV, became such an important world stage that political gestures, whether peaceful or tragically violent like the massacre of the Israeli team at the 1972 Olympics in Munich, became an ever-present possibility.

The Black Power salute at the 1968 Olympic Games is probably the only protest in Mexico City that the world remembers. Yet 10 days before the start of the Games the military opened fire on 10,000 people protesting against the Mexican regime and its spending vast sums on the Games when the country could ill afford it. More than 260 were killed and 1200 injured in the five hour battle. What wasn't seen on TV *couldn't* be important.

But protest was not the only political gesture. In July 1969 millions saw live on TV an eloquent demonstration of US

supremacy in the world of technology when their man stepped on the moon.

In the world of entertainment, broadcasting aided and reflected the transnational flow. In the 1950s, **Elvis Presley** became a symbol throughout the world of the new and infinitely expanding youth market that the radio, film and record industries were able to exploit. By the mid-1960s the one-way flow of music from the US was partly reversed by the fantastic popularity of the **Beatles** and the **Rolling Stones**.

Some singers and groups came to be seen as overwhelmingly threatening to the social order. At first it was just their images – long hair, oddly cut or casual clothes. Soon it was their flamboyant lifestyles – sex, violence and drugs – that caused a furore. And apart from lifestyles some music – for example **Bob Dylan's** 'protest songs' – was explicitly created to change opinion.

In 1967, the Beatles inaugurated the first worldwide live satellite link-up on TV with the hopeful 'All You Need Is Love'.

♪ "LOVE LOVE LOVE...
"...THAT IS ALL YOU NEED..."

HEY, MAN! YOU GOT THAT **DOORS** TAPE?

Despite commercial exploitation, such music still struck a chord of discontent both in Europe and America.

In less than two decades the assumed threat posed by pop music has been reversed. Images of starvation are now seen on TV to the sounds of the 1980s (many of them made by the stars of the 1960s). The capitalist world positively encourages its people to put **Band-Aid** on the wounds it continues to inflict on the Third World.

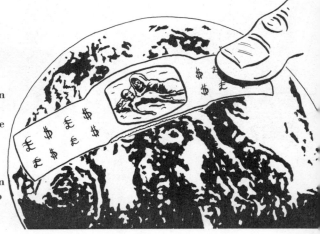

Chapter 4
SKY WARS

THE TECHNOLOGY that allowed television to become an international stage is the communications satellite. Its development was due to the same forces that pushed Marconi's inventions in the first place – **the demands of the military.**

1945. World War Two ended with a bang: two bangs to be precise – the atomic bombs dropped on Hiroshima and Nagasaki. 1945 also saw the first practical use of the electronic computer, **ENIAC**, and the prediction, in *Wireless World*, of the possibilities for trans-global communications inherent in the use of geo-stationary satellites. Its author has since become famous as the SF writer, **Arthur C. Clarke.**

A satellite fired into a high orbit 22,300 miles from Earth exactly matches our rotation, so it remains stationary in respect of a point on the Earth's surface. This makes it ideal for reception and transmission of radio/TV signals over a maximum portion of the Earth's surface. Three such satellites could cover the entire globe.

The technology to place and operate such satellites did not exist when Clarke wrote, but in 1944 the Germans had shown the shape of things to come when they succeeded in dropping V2 rocket bombs on London thanks to the skill of a team of gifted scientists led by **Werner von Braun.** The US occupying forces lost no time in getting hold of Von Braun and as many numbers of his group as they could. Most of the rest went to Russia.

Rocket propulsion, nuclear warheads and computerised guidance systems thenceforward became essential components of the **Cold War**. The super-power arms race which has continued ever since the late 1940s has been utterly dependent on (and at the same time a stimulant to) developments in electronics. **Every household name which shared in the post-war boom in electric and electronic consumer durables — Marconi, Phillips, Decca, Westinghouse, General Electric, AT & T — was also deeply implicated in the arms race and to a very great extent dependent on military contracts.**

This could be useful ... The year's 1947 and SHOCKLEY, BARDAIN and BRITTAIN have just tested their *TRANSISTOR*!!

... so AWAY with those expensive and weighty wireless valves! Radio receivers can be lighter, more portable, using **smaller, cheaper** batteries. What we need now is a **larger, cheaper** workforce to produce them!

Race you
up there !

The space race has furthered the development of communications satellites in all kinds of ways. The ability to put heavier and heavier payloads into orbit, and the need both to control precisely the movements and attitudes of satellites and to develop compact and economical energy sources, led to technological solutions which have followed as the inevitable consequence of the decision of the two super-powers not to be left behind in the space race. The objectives are political and military supremacy; **the global TV system, relying on satellite communication, is merely a spin-off.**

26m. diameter

AERIAL I , GOONHILLY, CORNWALL, BUILT TO RECEIVE TELSTAR'S SIGNALS IN 1962. PRIME CONTRACTOR OF LATER AERIALS WAS MARCONI COMMUNICATION SYSTEMS LTD.

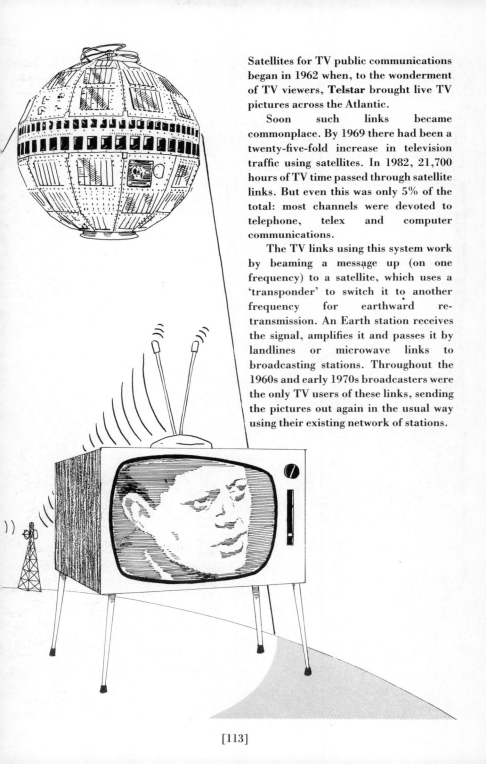

Satellites for TV public communications began in 1962 when, to the wonderment of TV viewers, **Telstar** brought live TV pictures across the Atlantic.

Soon such links became commonplace. By 1969 there had been a twenty-five-fold increase in television traffic using satellites. In 1982, 21,700 hours of TV time passed through satellite links. But even this was only 5% of the total: most channels were devoted to telephone, telex and computer communications.

The TV links using this system work by beaming a message up (on one frequency) to a satellite, which uses a 'transponder' to switch it to another frequency for earthward re-transmission. An Earth station receives the signal, amplifies it and passes it by landlines or microwave links to broadcasting stations. Throughout the 1960s and early 1970s broadcasters were the only TV users of these links, sending the pictures out again in the usual way using their existing network of stations.

But in 1975 the broadcasters suddenly found they had competition in the satellite states from an old rival – cable.

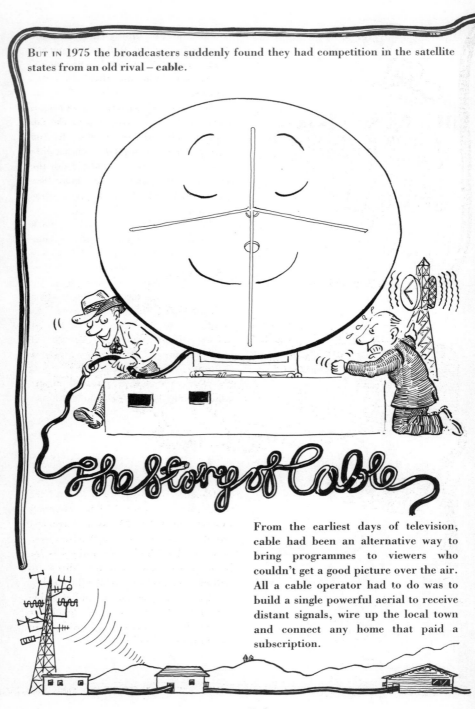

The Story of Cable

From the earliest days of television, cable had been an alternative way to bring programmes to viewers who couldn't get a good picture over the air. All a cable operator had to do was to build a single powerful aerial to receive distant signals, wire up the local town and connect any home that paid a subscription.

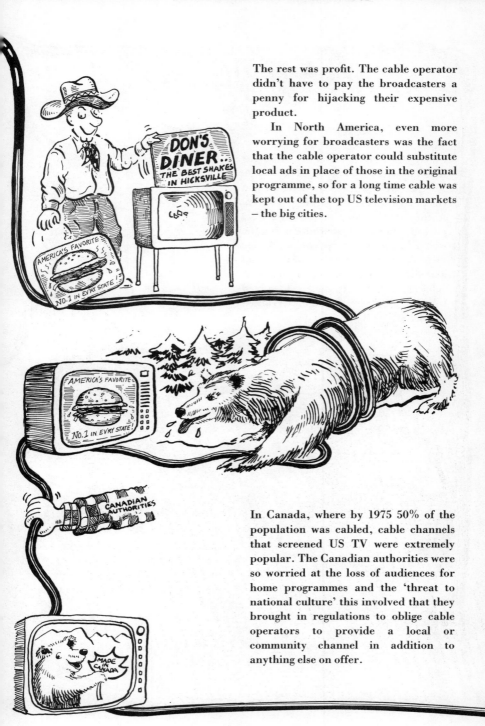

The rest was profit. The cable operator didn't have to pay the broadcasters a penny for hijacking their expensive product.

In North America, even more worrying for broadcasters was the fact that the cable operator could substitute local ads in place of those in the original programme, so for a long time cable was kept out of the top US television markets – the big cities.

In Canada, where by 1975 50% of the population was cabled, cable channels that screened US TV were extremely popular. The Canadian authorities were so worried at the loss of audiences for home programmes and the 'threat to national culture' this involved that they brought in regulations to oblige cable operators to provide a local or community channel in addition to anything else on offer.

Pay TV

About this time North American cable began to see the emergence of **pay-TV**, a system in which specially-formed companies bought up the rights to feature movies and supplied them in packages to cable systems for screening on a separate pay-channel. Cable viewers could only unscramble the signal and enjoy the movie by paying an extra subscription. The principal attraction was that the movies weren't interrupted by ads.

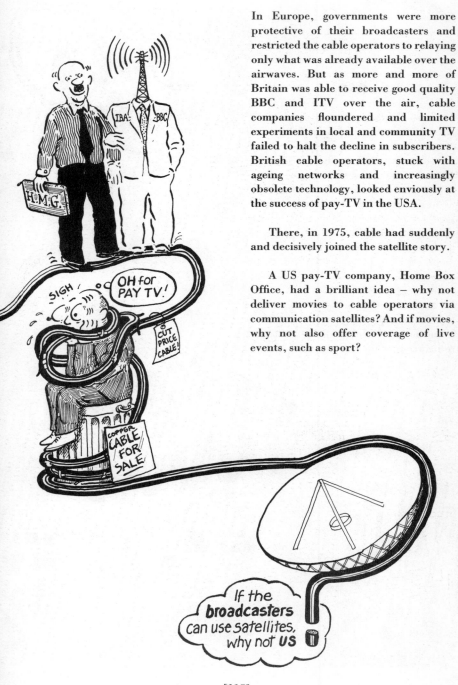

In Europe, governments were more protective of their broadcasters and restricted the cable operators to relaying only what was already available over the airwaves. But as more and more of Britain was able to receive good quality BBC and ITV over the air, cable companies floundered and limited experiments in local and community TV failed to halt the decline in subscribers. British cable operators, stuck with ageing networks and increasingly obsolete technology, looked enviously at the success of pay-TV in the USA.

There, in 1975, cable had suddenly and decisively joined the satellite story.

A US pay-TV company, Home Box Office, had a brilliant idea – why not deliver movies to cable operators via communication satellites? And if movies, why not also offer coverage of live events, such as sport?

It was a bold step because few cable operators at that time had the dishes to receive such signals. But Home Box Office's gamble paid off handsomely – the service created a demand and the price of dishes dropped. What had previously been a myriad of unconnected district cable systems could now be a very attractive *national* market for advertisers.

The first cable operator to see the potential of this was **Ted Turner**, whose WBS, Atlanta, began in December 1976 to transmit local sports events via satellite. It made him a fortune. Cable operators paid Turner for the signal on a 'per subscriber' basis – a few cents a month for each subscriber on their system. On top of this he scooped advertising revenues.

Satellite-delivered services so transformed the prospects for cable that it was now a case of too much traffic for the capacity of the older types of cable.

FIBRE OPTICS..

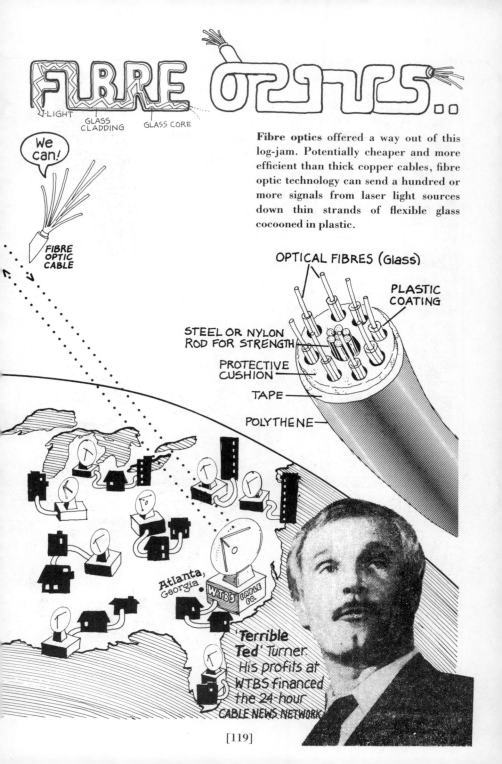

LIGHT · GLASS CLADDING · GLASS CORE

We can!

FIBRE OPTIC CABLE

Fibre optics offered a way out of this log-jam. Potentially cheaper and more efficient than thick copper cables, fibre optic technology can send a hundred or more signals from laser light sources down thin strands of flexible glass cocooned in plastic.

OPTICAL FIBRES (Glass)

PLASTIC COATING

STEEL OR NYLON ROD FOR STRENGTH

PROTECTIVE CUSHION

TAPE

POLYTHENE

Atlanta, Georgia

WTBS CABLE CO.

'Terrible Ted' Turner. His profits at WTBS financed the 24-hour CABLE NEWS NETWORK

[119]

Such a powerful facility as fibre optic technology means that far more than entertainment channels can be involved, and the traffic can be two-way. As well as choosing from a wide selection of TV channels subscribers could be linked to banks and shops, libraries and businesses. Computerised switching systems, like telephone exchanges only more sophisticated, could connect supply with demand and log the use of each service, deliver bills and monitor gas and electricity consumption, and even act as a remote burglar and fire alarm. As the use of home computers grows, these too could be linked to the network.

For those who wish to see this broadband inter-active network introduced, there are some crucial steps that have to be taken.

The technology needs to be developed beyond the experimental stage.

Every Western industrialised country with an electronics industry would like to be the first to mass produce components in order to create jobs at home and win sales abroad.

Who is to instal and operate the system that will usher in the wired society?

Until recently, telecommunications has been dominated by state-franchised monopolies or post offices. But in Reagan's USA and Thatcher's Britain a belief in unregulated competition and market forces has led to the dismantling of AT&T's monopoly in the USA and the privatisation of British Telecom.

How will this massive development be financed?

In Britain, a Conservative government decided that the public's appetite for more TV would bring private cable companies the profit they needed to re-equip with the new technology. The hoped-for information society was to be 'entertainment-led'; but despite hasty legislation and a minimum of regulation, the promised gold-rush didn't happen.

Partly this was due to the high development cost of the new technology; partly due to caution among the financial backers, and partly to the influence of the broadcasters. Broadcasters had good reason to be worried by cable expansion.

A **DISTRESSED** BROADCASTER

A **CABLE-SATELLITE** CONGLOMERATE IN **BULLISH** FORM

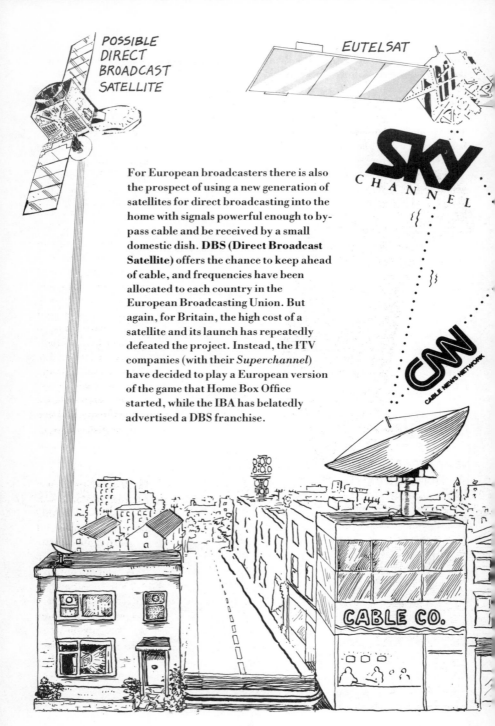

POSSIBLE DIRECT BROADCAST SATELLITE

EUTELSAT

SKY CHANNEL

CNN CABLE NEWS NETWORK

For European broadcasters there is also the prospect of using a new generation of satellites for direct broadcasting into the home with signals powerful enough to by-pass cable and be received by a small domestic dish. **DBS (Direct Broadcast Satellite)** offers the chance to keep ahead of cable, and frequencies have been allocated to each country in the European Broadcasting Union. But again, for Britain, the high cost of a satellite and its launch has repeatedly defeated the project. Instead, the ITV companies (with their *Superchannel*) have decided to play a European version of the game that Home Box Office started, while the IBA has belatedly advertised a DBS franchise.

CABLE CO.

INTELSAT V

The plan is now to lease channels on internationally-controlled low-powered communications satellites (that is, satellites primarily used for telephone and telex links) and transmit packaged services for reception by cable operators and redistribution to subscribers. In fact, improvements in satellite technology at both the transmission and reception ends are lowering the cost and size of the dish required.

In Britain, under new legislation you don't even need to be a cable operator to pick up and distribute satellite services. For a one-off £10 fee, you can obtain a SMA-TV licence (Satellite Master Antenna) and bring down into your hotel or café the latest European Cup match screened live by Italian television or Ted Turner's 24-hour news service from Atlanta, Georgia.

Top left: Robert Maxwell
Top right: Ted Turner
Bottom left: Rupert Murdoch
Bottom right: Silvio Berlusconi

With so many satellite TV services already in operation, governments are beginning to realise that exclusive financing of their own DBS operation may be too expensive. In consequence, alliances are being sought. **Robert Maxwell** and **Silvio Berlusconi** may have been rejected by the French government but they will doubtless find another government to work with. National services such as ITV's Superchannel are seeking to lease time on commercial satellites.

IF YOU CAN'T BEAT 'EM, JOIN 'EM!

...OR FLOG 'EM A FEW PROGRAMMES!

ITV

BBC

BBC ENTERPRISES

But satellite broadcasting also arouses serious political fears. Will we be trodden on by the 'footprint' of another nation's satellite? And Third World countries are worried that by the time they can afford satellite launches all the prime sites on the geo-stationary arc (and the frequencies to go with them) will be occupied by satellites owned by the rich countries.

These countries are able to exploit their technological advantage over poorer ones by unrestricted transmission of their own propaganda.

US Embassies have been equipped with receiving dishes so that senior government officials can perform to selected journalists assembled for 'interactive press conferences' in studios round the world. The first of these 'interactives' had **Jean Kirkpatrick**, representative to the UN, explaining why the US felt obliged to invade Grenada.
Colleagues were thrilled. 'Keep up the good work' – George P. Schultz. 'Enthusiastic about this dramatic new device to reach people abroad' – H. Kissinger. 'Seven million people in Italy alone!' – Secretary of State for Treasury.

The US also uses satellite time to transmit *America Today*, two hours daily of arts and sport ('not overt propaganda') which, being free, is gobbled up by cable systems. The BBC and ITN also use this material, and without telling viewers that it is provided free of charge by the Information Agency of a foreign government. 'I wouldn't have thought that necessary', said an ITN spokesperson.

Apart from the direct political threat, will satellites and cable offer us more choice and a better quality of programmes? It's very likely that they won't. Public broadcasting institutions such as the BBC will be under pressure to ditch their minority interest and controversial programmes in favour of audience-pulling shows.

The fear is that unrelieved mediocrity – a transnational bland diet – will be what everyone sees the world over.

48 TIMES THE USUAL JUNK?

WHAT we are now witnessing is a *convergence* of a range of formerly separate activities connected with leisure, work and the development of military weapons. Brought together these systems spell **IT – Information Technology** – and they converge on the home, which has become both a 'multi-function work station' and the point of sale and consumption of goods and cultural products.

So it's not only from TV screens and radio sets that this same diet will be offered us. Videos, films, records, paperbacks, magazines, newspapers, free sheets are increasingly coming from the same few owners. Five companies control 62.5% of the UK record market, six film distributors control over 90% of film rental, and virtually all cinemas belong to just two companies. 74% of newspapers are controlled by only three groups. Rupert Murdoch, as we have already mentioned, has interests not only in Skychannel but also in an international chain of newspapers, TV and radio stations. Similarly, **Robert Maxwell** has added cable and satellite services to his publishing (Pergamon), printing (BPCC), and newspaper (The Mirror Group) concerns.

This pattern is repeated and magnified in a world in which US-based multi-nationals occupy the dominant position.

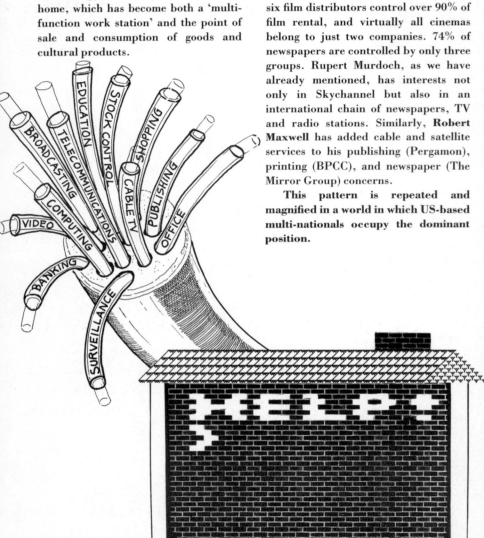

BUT how do the 'blessings' of
advanced civilization strike
Third World countries?
Escaping from colonial
relationships into
'independence', most
have found themselves
trapped by an economic
dependence which is
clearly reflected in their
media histories.
What follows is one
such history, a
fictional assembly
based on many real
life examples, from
the imaginary state of
Southia – a former
British colony.

The STORY of SOUTHIA

THE **REPUBLIC OF SOUTHIA** IS A LARGE ISLAND STATE IN THE MIDDLE OF THE TROPICS.

BEFORE THE SECOND WORLD WAR, SOUTHIA'S ONLY RADIO CAME FROM LONDON, THE COLONIAL CAPITAL, AS PART OF ITS OVERSEAS SERVICE.

MUST BE TIME FOR THE HAYDN CONCERT, DEAR.

AFTER WORLD WAR II, A SMALL LOCAL RADIO SERVICE STARTED ADOPTING THE LONDON MODEL.

THESE TECHNICIANS HAVE BEEN FULLY TRAINED IN LONDON...

HMM... WE'LL STILL HAVE TO KEEP A **SHARP EYE** ON THEM...

STUDIO
SILENCE ON ENTERING

RADIO SOUTHIA'S PRO-GRAMMES WERE MAINLY IN ENGLISH WITH ONLY SMALL SEGMENTS EACH DAY IN TWO OF THE MAIN LOCAL LANGUAGES.

[131]

ONE DAY, A COUP OCCURS IN NEIGHBOURING **EASTIA**...

AT A **NEWS AGENCY** HEADQUARTERS IN LONDON...

WHAT'S THE REACTION IN SOUTHIA TO THE EASTIAN COUP?

I DON'T WANT TO LOSE THIS!!

A SOUTHIAN FREELANCE JOURNALIST CONTACTS THE REGIONAL NEWS-DESK OF THE AGENCY.

I'VE HEARD THAT THE PRESIDENT IS GOING TO MAKE AN IMPORTANT ANNOUNCEMENT.

WE'RE ONLY INTERESTED IN THE STORY IF HE'S GOING TO COMMENT ON EASTIA.

OH, I'M **SURE** HE WILL!

[136]

[137]

Satellites provide yet another example of the way 'the free flow of communication' works to disadvantage the Third World counties. For them, transborder data flow is a matter of great concern. It can take the form either of the passage of data over a direct satellite link from a national branch of a corporation to its headquarters in the USA. Or by such satellites as Landsat 4 which can analyse agricultural and mineral resources in such detail that fieldcrops can be itemised.

Countries like Southia have cause to be aggrieved at the way the world's wealth is unevenly shared between the North and the South. **The raw deal it gets in broadcasting and communications is just a reflection of the basic economic disparity, which in turn is both symptom and consequence of the Cold War policies of the Superpowers.**

Southia was an invention but here are some genuine examples of the imbalance in media flow and resources taken from the UNESCO report *Many Voices, One World*, known as the *MacBride Report*.

*Associated Press sends 90,000 words daily from New York to Asia on its world wire service. In return Asia files a mere 19,000 words for worldwide distribution.

*Agence France-Presse (AFP) sends 30,000 words daily to Asia and receives 8000 words in return.

*A study of one particular day's news in Venezuela in 1977 showed that for every 100 items received from the USA, Venezuelan sources dispatched only 7 – and these via AP or UPI, both US agencies.

At this global level, decisions made in the boardrooms of communications moguls such as Rupert Murdoch have more influence than those of a cabinet meeting.

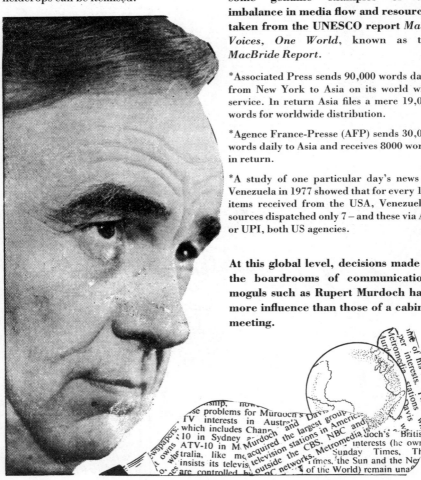

nued ownershi... ...per interests. Two of ... Metromedia stations whi... ...avis ...ip, now... ...se problems for Murdoch's Davis... TV interests in Austra... and the largest group... which includes Chan... ...acquired the largest group... 10 in Sydney... television stations in America... owns ATV-10 in M... outside the CBS, NBC and... tralia, like m... ...works. Metromedia... ...interests (he owns... insists its televis... ...Times, the Sun and the Ne... Sunday Times, Th... are controlled by... ...of the World) remain una... British...

Chapter 5
SEEING THROUGH THE MEDIA

So far we've looked at the increasingly important influence of media, especially TV, on national cultures and politics.

Clearly advertisers and politicians believe broadcasting is effective or they wouldn't spend vast sums on media campaigns. And if advertising – commercial or political – works, what else does?

Conservative politicians and moral re-armers would have us believe that there is a causal connection between sex, swearing, vandalism, violence, or whatever, on the screen and behaviour in real life.

These simplified explanations have a long history…

IN THE 1930s, the Nazis, as we've seen, enthused about the power of radio and film to indoctrinate the masses. A group of dissident marxist intellectuals working in Frankfurt, including **Herbert Marcuse** and **Theodor Adorno**, foresaw in such a use of the media new and terrifying possibilities for control. They were no less pessimistic in a society that was not an overtly totalitarian one – their newly adopted home of America.

Mass media debase culture and society, nein?

WELL, LET'S SEE...

WE INTERRUPT THIS BROADCAST TO ANNOUNCE A MARTIAN INVASION!!

WOW! IS THAT a FACT?!

The views of the Frankfurt School seemed to be strikingly confirmed by what happened in New York in 1939. **Orson Welles's** adaptation of the H.G. Wells story, *War of the Worlds*, used the vivid device of a fake news bulletin to announce the Martian invasion. Within minutes of the start of the broadcast thousands of listeners crowded the roads in a panic escape from the city.

[142]

But on the whole the Americans regarded themselves as sturdy-independents-in-the-land-of-the-free. By the time they'd won World War Two and launched the Cold War, they weren't inclined to think of themselves as lemmings. Instead of adopting the Frankfurt School's deep pessimism, the academics condemned the boundless claims for broadcasting made by the politicians and advertisers.

Social scientists busied themselves on media output's direct effects: the influence of party political broadcasts on voting intentions prior to elections, marketing campaigns on consumers preferences, and whether children shown 'violent' films – generally of other children beating up inflatable 'Bobo' dolls – felt compelled to copy what they saw.

A fairly consistent answer seemed to emerge: there are next to *no* media 'effects', not least because most people forget almost everything they have seen as soon as a programme has finished, or remember it very selectively. If media messages have any impact at all, it's not because they act like bullets from a gun; their influence must be very much more subtle than that.

Another important finding which added weight to this outlook was that members of an audience differ greatly in the way they react to the same programme:

they reject it...

they don't hear it...

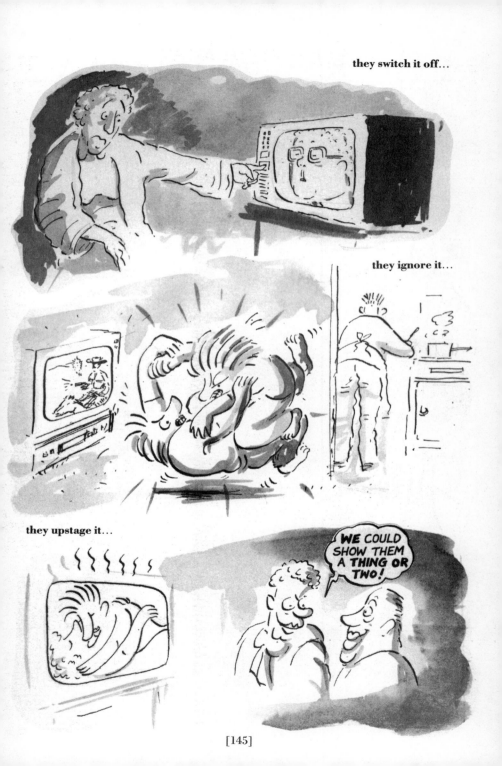

they switch it off…

they ignore it…

they upstage it…

WE COULD SHOW THEM A **THING** OR **TWO!**

[145]

Studies of the 'uses and gratifications' which people get from listening and viewing underlined both great differences in audience responses and the deep need many people have for radio and TV. For example, listeners described how the radio...

'takes my mind off other things'

'is like a friend calling in'

'helps to keep me cheerful'

'keeps my mind active'

'helps to keep me going'

'allows me to get involved in it'.

In a sentence, the virtual consensus declared that it's not so much what media do to people, as what people do with media.

But the question of media *effects* just wouldn't go away. When the USA was rocked in the 1960s by waves of violent protest, politicians decided it *had* to be television that was to blame.

It was hard to deny that TV and radio must be doing *something* to their audiences, particularly since so many people – especially the young – spent so much of their lives in front of them. By this time almost everyone owned one or more receivers and it had been calculated that, on average, children were watching TV for half as long again as they spent in the classroom. Even before starting school, children would have been 'exposed to' countless scenes of crime, sexual depravity, and violence.

Reporting in 1972, the central theme of the National Commission on the Causes and Prevention of Violence (known as the **Eisenhower Commission** after its Chairman, Milton Eisenhower) was that TV couldn't have it both ways: **if it sells products, it must also influence behaviour.**

One result of its report was a massive boost for mass communication research both in the USA and overseas. The colourful writings of the Canadian **Marshall McLuhan**, although often obscure (one critic described his style as 'a viscous fog through which loom stumbling metaphors'), were also highly provocative. Many of the expressions he coined soon became clichés, but they also reminded researchers to look less at the messages and more at the media that conveyed them.

The most obvious changes wrought were on life-styles. TV, for example, had become the favoured leisure activity of the majority of the population. People went out less, their sleep patterns were altered and eating schedules adjusted according to programming. The medium's soporific virtues were soon spotted by parents, who used TV as an electronic baby-sitter. (Mental hospitals, prisons and other long-stay institutions soon followed suit.)

Even public utilities were affected. Water system engineers had to accommodate the drop in pressure caused by toilet-flushing during commercial breaks, and power supplies needed to cope with the surge of demand when kettles are turned on.

But perhaps the most significant effect of TV, it was increasingly argued, does not result from particular programmes at all, but from the whole shift of entertainment, politics and general knowledge from the public to the private sphere.

What used to happen in pubs, launderettes, football terraces, community centres, and union and political meetings, is now part of a domestic experience. More than face to face experience or any other social institution, it is TV that entertains and informs. TV 'defines reality' and 'sets the agendas' – it says what the important issues of the day are, and who should be heard, marginalised, ignored, ridiculed or stereotyped. And further, the agenda TV constructs is overwhelmingly biased in favour of an 'Establishment' view of the world.

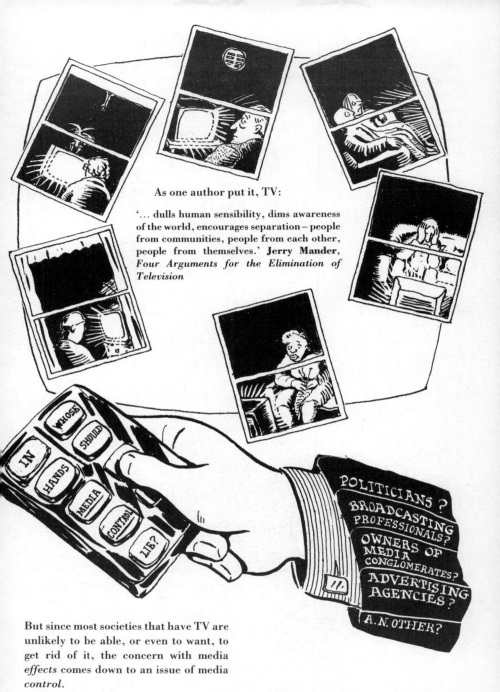

As one author put it, TV:

'... dulls human sensibility, dims awareness
of the world, encourages separation – people
from communities, people from each other,
people from themselves.' **Jerry Mander,**
Four Arguments for the Elimination of
Television

But since most societies that have TV are
unlikely to be able, or even to want, to
get rid of it, the concern with media
effects comes down to an issue of media
control.

The answer to some extent depends
on working out what forces determine
not just the overall structure but also the
detailed content of TV and radio.

[151]

THE STATE in every country attempts to restrict broadcasting, though in different ways and to very different extents. In Britain, for example, *direct* government control is rare (though not unknown; for example, programmes on the secret services have been banned). And given that broadcasters are ultimately dependent on government for their franchises and their funding it would perhaps not be surprising if the government-appointed boards of the BBC

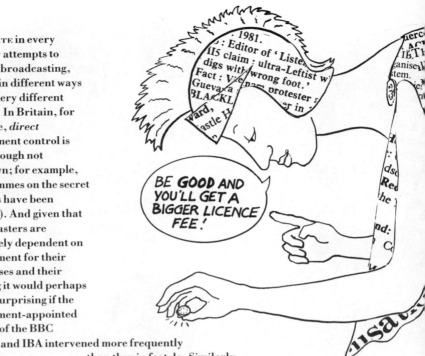

and IBA intervened more frequently than they in fact do. Similarly, in Britain (though not in the USA), companies have little *direct* power in determining the character of programmes that surround their adverts.

But there is no need to assume that all power in the organisation lies in the hands of a tiny elite locked into conspiracy with the rest of the ruling class. Nor do we have to assume systematic political bias among producers, editors and journalists, though it has come to light that all potential recruits to the BBC were security-vetted for their political views. On the contrary, **routine and unconscious practices** alone, even on the part of programme-makers with otherwise quite radical views, are an immensely powerful force in determining the outcomes. Why is this?

[152]

Self-censorship. Since producers or journalists don't expect to be able to make and show a programme in the way they would like, they don't even try.

Production standards. The demand for 'high quality', professionally-made programmes means that groups with something to say (but lacking a 'broadcast-standard' camera, video or tape-machine to record it on) will not be allowed to say it *for themselves* and in their own way. If they get any chance at all to be heard, they must have the 'experts' there to help them.

A related issue is, ironically enough, the 'professional ideology' (written into the broadcasting acts) that the broadcaster must observe 'due impartiality and accuracy'. This has generally been interpreted to mean that 'points of view' must be clearly signalled as such and immediately matched by an opposing view. Does this ensure that everybody gets a fair hearing? Far from it.

Recruitment. As a rule, the people who get hired are just like the people already in post, so the very people who are marginalised in the programmes, such as women and black people, are also barely represented in the organisation that produces the programmes.

Emphasising that rival 'opinions' are being expressed often makes them seem 'odd', curtails any development of the case and discourages the viewer from taking up the challenge by simply neutralising – cancelling out – the argument being put forward.

AND THOSE OF YOU **LATEBIRDS** WHO HAVE BEEN WATCHING THESE DISTURBING PICTURES OF POLICE BRUTALITY WILL BE ABLE TO HEAR THEIR REPLY AT THE **EARLIER** TIME OF EIGHT O'CLOCK ON **SATURDAY** NIGHT. THAT'S ALL FROM US TONIGHT... ... **GOODNIGHT!**

Furthermore, it is often taken for granted that the primary, or 'official' version of events should be that offered by the 'authorities' in the field (generally 'experts', police or government representatives, depending on the issue)...

HELLO, **TERRY** FROM WAPPING...

HALLO ROGER! UM, I JUST WANT TO SAY THAT THE MANAGING DIRECTOR WAS **NOWHERE NEAR** THE PICKET LINE... I WAS ON IT MYSELF AND THERE WAS **NO VIOLENCE!**

WELL, **TERRY**, WE DON'T KNOW WHO **YOU** ARE... DO YOU **REALLY** EXPECT US TO TAKE **YOUR** WORD AGAINST THE **MANAGING DIRECTOR'S**? ARE YOU SAYING THAT THE **MANAGING DIRECTOR** IS A **LIAR**?... NEXT CALLER PLEASE!!

...and that certain groups – for example those defined as 'terrorists', such as the IRA – are deemed to be so 'partial' that their voice should not be heard at all.

I'LL TELL YOU FELLAS SOMETHING... D'YOU WANNA KNOW HOW TO GET **PRIME TIME TV** FOR YOUR **ACT OF TERRORISM**? IT'S EASY...

... JUST CALL IT A **SURGICAL STRIKE**... **DOCTOR'S ORDERS** 'N' ALL THAT! **YES**? THE FELLA WITH THE RED TIE...

... **UH**, MR. PRESIDENT, **BOB SMITH, NETWORK NEWS**... DO YOU THINK IT HELPS BEING IN CHARGE OF THE WORLD'S RICHEST NATION?

... WHY, THAT'S A **GOOD QUESTION**, BOB, I'M GLAD YOU ASKED ME... YES, I GUESS IT **DOES**... NOW...THE LADY IN BLUE... **MY!** I'M SORRY, MARGARET...

TV journalists and editors act as 'gatekeepers': they give very few events any coverage at all, and keep the vast majority of events out. There is even considerable selection *within* an event.

JIM BAKER RESISTED **INTIMIDATION** BY **PICKETS** AS HE **RETURNED TO WORK** TODAY AT THE SHEFFIELD PLANT...

THE **NEWS**

NOT THE **NEWS**

DESPITE **HARASSMENT BY POLICE** AND **INTIMIDATION BY THE MEDIA,** 100,000 ARE **STILL ON STRIKE,** STRONGLY **SUPPORTED** BY THEIR **FAMILIES**...

Youth blamed police harassment for the 'riots' which took place in the U.K. in 1981, yet we were given less than a minute of TV for our explanations; the police had nearly **ten**!!

Many details and circumstances are deemed to be of little interest or relevance. Of course, it could hardly be otherwise – there are an awful lot of

things going on in the world. But what qualities are the programme makers looking for in an event before they believe it can 'work as a story'?

What are their 'news values'? A study by **Galtung** and **Ruge** in the USA in 1973 identified the following conditions which an event has to fulfil to be noticed *as* news...

A **NEWSWORTHY** EVENT...

THIS STORY IS FICTION BUT ITS TREATMENT IS TYPICAL

AN **UN**-NEWSWORTHY EVENT...

...IS **SLOW**...

NEWS

Good evening. The continued.

...**PREDICTABLE**...

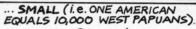

... racial discrimination, arrest, detention, torture, disappearances and extra-judicial killings...

..**NEGATIVE** IN CHARACTER ABOUT A COUNTRY WITH WHOM WE SEEK GOOD RELATIONS...

... by **Indonesian** troops...

... **SMALL** (i.e. ONE AMERICAN EQUALS 10,000 WEST PAPUANS)...

WEST PAPUA (IRIAN JAYA)

INDONESIA

AUSTRALIA

among the population of **West Papua**...

... IT MUST BE **UNABLE** TO FIT INTO EXISTING TYPES OF NEWS...

NEWS

... is believed to be in reprisal for...

... MUST **NOT** CONCERN TOP PEOPLE OR NATIONS...

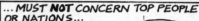

... a stubborn guerilla campaign by **Melanesians** resisting Indonesian occupation since 1969.

... MUST HAVE **NO** EFFECT OR RELEVANCE TO AUDIENCE ...

NEWS

Among six West Papuan women held without trial since 1980...

... IF POSSIBLE BE FOCUSED ON A FEMALE INDIVIDUAL WITH AN **UN**-PRONOUNCEABLE NAME FROM AN UNKNOWN 'ETHNIC MINORITY'...

NEWS

... is **Persila Yakadewa**..

... MUST ALREADY BE **UN**-NEWSWORTHY..

JAKARTA

INDONESIA

JAVA

Tonight there was still **no comment** from Jakarta.

... AND DEPENDS ON WHAT ELSE THERE IS IN THE BULLETIN...

NEWS

And, finally, women protesting against the siting of cruise missiles at Greenham **Common** again braved the cold...

THIS STORY IS FACT BUT ITS TREATMENT IS FICTION

Since as viewers, listeners and readers we *make* meaning as much as we receive it, how do different people *perceive* programmes? Do audiences respond to (or 'read') programmes in the way their producers intend? How much is ignored or even rejected? To what extent do people create alternative 'readings' of what they have seen?

... AND BEFORE THE NEXT CHAPTER, WHICH STARTS IN JUST A FEW MOMENTS, I'D LIKE YOU TO THINK ABOUT HOW YOU SEE **ME** ...
... AS A **PROGRESSIVE** FORCE: A BLACK WOMAN IN A POSITION OF AUTHORITY?
... OR AS A **REACTIONARY** FORCE: A BLACK WOMAN SERVICING WHITE MAN-MADE NEWS?
... OR AS A TOKEN GESTURE, DEFUSING THE PRESSURE FOR MORE EQUAL PARTICIPATION IN THE MEDIA?
... HOW DO I SEE **MYSELF**?

DO **ANY** OF US RECOGNISE OUR**SELVES** IN THE MEDIA?

MEDIA & POWER

Chapter 6 ANSWERING BACK

THE CONCENTRATION of ownership in modern communications, and their transnational scale, make them increasingly inaccessible to democratic control at the level of national government.

What can we do about this? If we sit and wait for a change of ownership and control we could wait for ever. If we surrender each medium which capitalism gets hold of and develops we'd soon be reduced to silence.

There are, in this wall-to-wall Dallas syndrome, still some spaces left and contradictions to be exploited. Paradoxically, the technologies of instant printing, cassette recording, radio transmission and video production developed by the multinationals also give opportunities for local democratic control and small-scale use. And that's important because hearts and minds can be won around issues that affect people directly and personally.

First of all, tell the broadcasters what you think!

Be sure of your facts. Note time and channel. You may want to wait till the end-credits or check in the *Radio Times* or *TV Times* for the name of the producer and, for ITV, the station that made the programme.

Telephone the IBA (01-584 7011) and ask for the Duty Officer. Call the local ITV station. The BBC's Duty Officer for radio is on 01-580 4468, for TV, 01-743 8000. You will be asked for your name, and perhaps what town or area you come from. There is no need to harangue, but be assertive and make certain your complaint is registered in the complaints log. It's worth doing: the log is seen next day by top management.

Telephoned support may help defend a programme or producer threatened with the chop.

STOP! WE'VE HAD A FAVOURABLE RESPONSE FROM A MEMBER OF THE PUBLIC!

IN YOUR PROGRAMME ABOUT THE NURSES' ACTION AGAINST HOSPITAL CLOSURES – CAN YOU WRITE THAT IN FULL, PLEASE? – YOU INTERVIEWED FOUR MANAGEMENT REPRESENTATIVES, TWO PATIENTS AND ONLY ONE NURSE...

If you have time, **write** – BBC and IBA addresses are available in reference libraries. Perhaps there is an advisory committee which corresponds to your interest. The BBC has 52 advisory bodies (listed in its yearly handbook, in reference libraries), and the IBA also has quite a few. Try writing to the chairperson of one or more of these. If it's an advertisement you are objecting to, write to the manufacturers and tell them you'll be boycotting their product.

It's equally important to **praise** something that's good.

THE INCLUSION OF LESBIANS AS WELL AS GAY MEN IN YOUR SERIES HAS BEEN A REAL STEP FORWARD....

welcome inclusion of lesbian and gay men but why must you show it at _midnight_?!!

Contact trade union members at the station. Ask them (or their union's head office) for their codes of practice and use their procedures to make a formal complaint. Keep your own union informed as well as the media unions. *You don't have to fight these battles on your own!*

MOTION PASSED BY 1982
TUC CONGRESS

Congress deplores the frequent representa-
tions through films, television
and t
of gr

It al
rece
Com
dard
inv
siv

Co
tre
wo
in

C
al
a
b
r
c

ACTT CODE OF PRACT
AGAINST SEXISM

INTRODUCTION
The ACTT is committed to eq
tw
se
b
e
b
c
v
e

NUJ Code of Condu

1. A journalist has
   highest pr
   standard

2. A journal.
   the principle c
   press and other i.
   collection of informati.
   expression of commen
   He/she shall strive to e
   distortion, news supp
   censorship.

3. A journalist shall stri
   the information he/sh
   fair and accurate, avc
   of comment and con
   established fact and
   distortion, selection
   misrepresentation.

4. A journalist shall re
   harmful inaccuraci
   correction and apo
   prominence and af
   reply to persons cr
   issue if of sufficier

5. A journalist shall
   photographs and
   straightforward r
   other means can
   over-riding cons
   public interest.
   entitled to exerc
   conscientious o
   such means.

Women contri
cial and

Contact the **Right of Reply Unit** at the Campaign for Press and Broadcasting Freedom for advice.

Some channels and programmes give you a chance of feedback on the air; for example, the BBC's Community Programme Unit currently produces *Open Space*. C4's *Right of Reply* may screen your use of their Video Box. Or your letter to BBC's *Point of View*, to Radio 4's *PM* or *Any Answers* may be read out.

Then there are **phone-ins** on national and local radio – it's important not to leave them to well-organised right wing groups. Their favoured tactic is to target a particular programme and to back each other up but without identifying their mutual affiliations. This makes it seem that the whole audience is of one mind on the question being debated.

Once you've written letters to a producer or to the local press, and spoken at meetings, **the broadcasters may come to you and ask for an interview.** Don't feel so flattered or honoured that you forget to ask some hard questions back.

If this approach doesn't lose you the interview, you may nevertheless find that the recorded result will be edited out of all recognition.

You can, of course, **make your own programmes.** You don't even need to own the technology or have the expertise – there are organisations set up to help you.

EXCUSE ME...
I UNDERSTAND
YOUR SON WAS
INJURED IN
LAST WEEK'S
RIOT....

WHAT **ORG-
ANISATION**
ARE YOU FROM?
WHAT IS YOUR
STATUS? CAN
YOU **DELIVER**
WHAT YOU
PROMISE? IS THE
PROGRAMME **LIVE**
OR **RECORDED**? WHEN
WILL IT BE **TRANSMITTED**?
WHO ELSE WILL BE ON
THE PROGRAMME? HOW
WILL YOU **INTRODUCE**
ME? IF YOU'RE RECORDING
THIS **HOW MUCH** ARE YOU
LIKELY TO **USE**? WHO
WILL **PRESENT** THE PRO-
GRAMME? WHAT **FEES**
OR **EXPENSES** ARE
AVAILABLE?... I'LL NEED
TO ARRANGE **CHILDCARE**.
CAN YOU SEND A **CAR** TO
PICK ME UP?

IF YOU'RE
A **VICTIM** OF
URBAN UNREST
WHY DON'T YOU
ACT LIKE ONE?

Towards the end of the 1960s the video portapak (light weight television equipment which had been developed for military airborne reconnaissance in the Vietnam War) became popular with radical activists.

Video shot on portable equipment can be replayed instantly to participants. (It's very different from the experience of using film, which can't be seen for several weeks until it's been processed.) With video, the camera operator can quickly learn to improve shooting techniques, the participants can check how they look and what they've said, and ask for a re-shoot if necessary. And of course tape can be rewound and reused, so it's relatively cheap.

Now that electronic processing can give picture quality good enough to transmit at broadcast standard, TV companies have no reason to exclude programmes on *technical* grounds. (They may still exclude them on *political* ones, though.)

British TV at present actually allows more space then radio to minority voices. Channel 4, though funded by advertising, is required by law to provide for 'tastes and interests' not generally served by ITV. And because it's cheaper to buy in programmes than to make them in-house, space has been created for **independent production companies**.

The radio and TV networks also have **Access** slots, chiefly for community groups to get a public hearing. The group is lent professional-standard equipment and the technicians to use them. After its broadcast, the programme can be used as a video to continue publicising the group's activities.

But there are many obvious problems. Slots are few, the programmes often look 'amateurish', and are scheduled for transmission at times when audiences need to make a special effort to watch.

GOOD EVENING – OR GOOD MORNING, I SHOULD SAY. IF YOU HAVEN'T TURNED OFF YOUR SETS ALREADY, WELCOME TO THIS PRO-GRAMME BY THE **CAMPAIGN FOR BETTER ACCESS SLOTS**. IT'S THE FIRST IN A **SHORT** SEA-SON OF **LOW-BUDGET** PRO-GRAMMES BY **MINORITY** GROUPS. WE APOLOGISE FOR THE **MONO-TONOUS TONE** AND **HUMOUR-LESS NATURE** OF THIS BROADCAST BUT ASK YOU TO UNDERSTAND THAT THIS IS THE ONLY CHANCE WE'RE GOING TO GET TO EXPRESS OUR VIEWS ON **TV** LIKE THIS AND IT MAKES US FEEL **NERVOUS** IN CASE WE DON'T MAKE OUR POINT CLEAR, SO THAT'S WHY WE'RE **VERY SERIOUS** AND DON'T TAKE ANY **RISKS**. IS ANYONE STILL WATCHING.... ?

This leads to the justifiable complaint that the programmes mainly preach to the converted. Some critics go further. Access slots may look good when it comes to a TV company's franchise being renewed, but they're no substitute for sharing power.

Access slots fall between stools. Some prefer to keep control over the whole programme and make it themselves, others prefer to go direct to the network producers. What you can lose in control you can make up for in impact and audience size.

So FAR we've looked at the spaces within the existing media which allow us to participate — with varying degrees of success — in what it produces. But there are other spaces too. For as long as governments have sought to control the frequency spectrum individuals and groups have claimed a right to their share. Earlier we saw how amateur experimenters were crucial to the development of broadcasting. Now we look at their descendants, and those who, legally or illegally, have asserted their right to make their own broadcasts independent of either state or commercial interests.

With TV this history is brief...

In **ITALY**, following political crisis and protest against state control of broadcasting, **deregulation** of TV and radio in the early '70's allowed a rash of independent TV stations. Today there are about 400 private **local TV** stations, mostly served by US programming. Those which started as community interest stations have fallen by the wayside or are prey for commercial predators.

In **HOLLAND**, a non-commercial public service system provides technical facilities and co-ordinates the output of openly biased programme-making associations, based on the country's main religious and political divisions. The amount of airtime each group has is dependent on the number of its subscribers. 10% of airtime is available for small minority groups.

London's first pirate TV station has begun regular weekly broadcasts to a claimed .... of some 50,000 viewers living .... Brixton. The illegal ....

In the **UK**, in 1986, a pirate TV station run by a collective of independent film-makers took to the air, aiming to encourage government de-regulation of the airwaves, Italian-style, and the growth of **local/low power TV**.

"WE PROPOSE OUR SOUNDS AND IMAGES. WHAT THE VIEWERS DO WITH THEM IS THEIR CONCERN, NOT OURS."

In the **USA**, licensed amateurs can transmit to each other or to Amateur Television (ATV) clubs for amplification and re-transmission to a wider audience. In the UK, members of the British Amateur Television Club number about 2,500. They are the inheritors of a tradition of amateur transmission, begun many years ago with the invention of **RADIO**, to which we now turn.....

For years, **HAM RADIO** or **SHORTWAVE ENTHUSIASTS** have communicated with one another throughout the world.

INTERNATIONAL Amateur Radio

HMM! WEATHER'S GOOD! I MIGHT TRY GOING TO **JAPAN**...

CQ! CQ!

To get a **CALL SIGN** and a **licence** to broadcast, amateurs must pass examinations in radio theory and practice.

Like Marconi, whose first interest was that his invention should save lives at sea, amateur radio operators have been vital in providing disaster communications – for instance, between earthquake-ravaged Mexico City and the outside world in September 1985.

Hams' sputtering signals tell how bad it is

From Patt Morrison in Los Angeles

Some of Mexico's 1,820 licensed ham radio operators, who normally use their hobby as a sort of electronic pen-pal system, suddenly became a primary link between central Mexico and the outside world on Thursday.

For about 12 hours after the earthquake played crack-the-whip with the buildings and boulevards of Mexico City, the sputtering signals sent through the high, thin air from a variety of ham radio sets were letting the world know bad it had been

and forth from his ham set to the television or portable radio, passing along the latest news, and then patiently spelling and respelling his name over and over for news organisations.

He paused for a linkup with his son, Frank Jr, in Texas, to reassure him that all was well in Guadalupe Lake, and took a call from a Florida father worried about his daughter, who was honeymooning in Mazatlan. All he could do was

The amateurs can find their initial broadcasts of a tragedy picked up by the mainstream media networks and transmitted worldwide.

A **CITIZENS'**
BAND (**CB**) radio,
or **rig**, can
transmit as well as
receive.

Although CB has been established in the US since
1947, in the UK 'breakers' were broadcasting to one
another long before the government legalised their equipment or allocated a frequency. By 1981, more than **sixty**
countries, including the UK, had legalised CB.

In a way both ham radio and CB have been **ghetto**-ised as
hobbies for a narrow group of interests or as useful point-to-
point communications. They have little to do with **broadcasting**
in the sense of groups **disseminating programmes** to each
other. But, in America, a tradition of **community radio**
stations has developed to do precisely this.

USA 1949...

U.S. RADIO WAS **SUNK** IN A **SLOUGH** OF **COMMERCIAL DESPOND**. BUT OVER IN **CALIFORNIA**...

Operated by ex-WW2 veteran, Lew Hill, **KPFA** aired subjects considered so 'un-American' that they were never heard elsewhere.

The Berkeley station was the first in the world to be financed by subscriptions from listeners. Later...

During the 1960s, when civil rights, Vietnam and the women's movement became issues, other community stations followed. Protected by '**freedom of speech**', people would build a station, apply for a licence and run it themselves, raising the money through subscriptions and grants.

> We've got the transmitter working!

> Someone's donated their entire collection of Brazilian folk recordings!

> I'm getting time off work this week to finish the soundproofing.

> How's our training schedule going?

> My health group's going to do some programmes.

> So now all we need are a few more nails and a licence!

Now there are at least fifty community radio stations in the U.S.

In **Canada** an enlightened government positively **encouraged** stations to be set up to serve **distant communities** which the Canadian Broadcasting Corporation (C.B.C.) couldn't reach.

ᐳᓄᒃ ᐁᑕᕐ ᐃᐊᕐᐅᐊᐳ

7 INUKTITUT RULES O.K.!

In the early 1970s, they went further. Urban community radio stations were licenced to serve **ethnic** and **other groups** not otherwise catered for.

VANCOUVER CO-OP RADIO

CO-OP RADIO 102.7FM
PROGRAMME GUIDE · OCTOBER

10.00 am **Short People** A show by and for kids

7.30 **THE LESBIAN SHOW** Oct 11: How much do we have in common with male homosexuals?

7.15 **LIVE FROM CITY HALL** City Council

But the move to develop community radio was not confined to North America. In 1975, the lack of **fine** (classical) **music** on **Australian** state and commercial stations enabled a group in Sydney to get a special licence.

Since that time 30 public stations have been established in Australia.

In **ITALY**, in the early 1970s, hundreds of **'radios librés'** burst upon the airwaves, exploiting a constitutional loophole. A High Court ruling decreed that the State broadcasting organisation, **RAI**, did **not** have a monopoly at a local level, so anyone could broadcast who could find a spare frequency.

Most stations that took advantage of this were commercial, little more than **juke-boxes of the air** and outlets for the business interests whose control over central government was being displaced.

But a few stations challenged the conservative bias of RAI, giving **access** to **radical left views** and **unorthodox formats.**

In March 1977, **Radio Alice** in Bologna was raided by police for allegedly inciting a riot...

THE POLICE HAVE COME IN... WE'VE GOT OUR HANDS UP... THEY'RE RIPPING AWAY THE MIKE !!

French broadcasting, run entirely by the state until recently, was opposed by radios librés from 1977. **Jamming** and **police raids** harassed the stations except where **local political support** was strong.

In **Longwy, Lorraine**, where thousands of steelworkers were made redundant, two stations defied the government for over a year with the support of the mayor and trade unions...

In May 1981, the **Socialists** were returned to power and allowed **free radio broadcasting** subject to certain conditions (no advertisements, limitations on power, etc.). **Result: 113 stations in Paris alone** by Christmas 1981. The situation threatened to become as chaotic as in Italy.

Regulation was introduced to limit the choice in the capital to 20 stations. The decisions of the regulatory commission as to which free radio stations should get which frequencies similarly reduced the numbers in France as a whole...

BELGIUM's free radio explosion began in 1978 with stations springing up to contest **environmental** issues. Although many stations have gone commercial there is a thriving sector of **democratic** radio in the KPFA tradition. At *Radio Air Libre*, Brussels, "a different voice in the jungle of the airwaves", an elected management committee makes the day-to-day decisions and answers to a general assembly meeting once a fortnight...

In all these stations, the essential feature is **democratic control** by listeners and workers (paid and volunteer) and users of the station, exercised ultimately in meetings or general assemblies which can vote the management in or out of office. Typically, **voting rights** can be earned through a probationary period of work in the station, either making programmes or helping with fund-raising or administration, or through payment of an annual subscription and/or a minimum attendance at meetings.

In the **UK**, there has been no tradition of community broadcasting, except in very restricted conditions:

STUDENT RADIO stations, their signals confined to campus, (unlike their counterparts in North America and Australia)

HOSPITAL RADIO, reaching patients on closed-circuit systems...

We aint no threat 'cos we're **ANGELS**...

Gosh! What a shame no-one heard our **RAG-WEEK** special!

FIGHT NHS CLOSURES

... and a handful of **CABLE RADIO STATIONS**, chafing at the restrictions of being confined to cable.

Twice, though, **RADIO PIRACY** has been successful in changing government policy...

1964...

CAN'T BUY ME LO-OVE!

Pirates took to the air from boats anchored just outside territorial waters, forced by state control to operate illegally. It was unlicensed **commercial** broadcasting, heavily financed by the music industry, but also by small firms who couldn't afford or wouldn't need national or even regional advertising for their garage or restaurant. **Radio Caroline** and **Radio London** met demands for current music styles that the BBC wouldn't satisfy.

In 1967 the state suppressed this first wave of piracy through the Marine Offences Act which outlawed supplying or advertising on ship radio stations. But the popularity of the pirates forced a change of policy on a reluctant government and BBC. 'Wunnerful' Radio 1 was created, a service of largely pop music presented by DJs poached from the pirates.

The BBC had already set up its own **LOCAL RADIO STATIONS**, and, encouraged by the pirates' popularity, the Conservative government authorised **COMMERCIAL RADIO** under the Independent Broadcasting Authority in 1973.

CAN'T BUY ME LO— GLUG!!

BBC WUNNERFUL RADIO 1

BBC LOCAL RADIO

COMMERCIAL RADIO

Under the **BBC, LOCAL RADIO** has come at the bottom in the pile of priorities. Station budgets have been cut – so the staff time to help **COMMUNITY ACCESS** has disappeared – and coverage areas have been expanded. BBC's 30 local radio stations are now more **regional** than local.

"WE TAKE VERY SERIOUSLY INDEED OUR RESPONSIBILITIES TO ENTERTAIN, EDUCATE AND INFORM..."

"AND WE LOOK FORWARD TO **SERVING THE COMMUNITY** WHEREVER WE CAN..."

BUT **NOT THAT AGGRESSIVE COMMUNITY RADIO LOBBY WHO INSIST ON CALLING US COMMERCIAL RATHER THAN INDEPENDENT!**

"A radio station that talks marketing has got to be worth listening to."

SEVERN SOUND

Hmmph!

TRADES COUNCIL

The tendency of some 50 **commercial** stations is to neglect the **local** in search of the **national**. Commercial radio teeters on the edge of financial disaster, despite being baled out by **multinational shareholdings.** Top 40 music and DJ patter make it difficult to distinguish one station from another, even though the IBA is charged by law to ensure "that the programmes broadcast from different stations.... in different localities do not consist of identical or similar material."

The IBA's selection and review of franchise applicants is secret, but the stations' published promises are not matched by their performance.

In **both** types of stations, it is the professionals who define the needs and say what counts as news. **IT'S NOT THE STUFF OF WHICH ACCESS IS MADE** and it's little wonder that in the late 1970s and 1980s fresh waves of **piracy**, this time on land, attempted to give listeners sounds and opinions local radio ignored...

DBC... From Brixton or whether Tottenham you have fe tune in to this yah rebel station...

This is **Sheffield Peace Radio**... bringing you alternative coverage of the peace issues...

SOUL

FUNK

K-JAZZ

LONDON GREEK RADIO

Gaywaves

Good morning, you're tuned to **Two Spires Radio**...right-wing radio for the Midlands!

GOSPEL

I'm getting tired of all these break-ins!

HOME OFFICE

DEPT. OF TRADE AND INDUSTRY

We must have raided that station 27 times!

Some of the pirates carried advertising and this threat to the ailing commercial sector finally forced the government into severe repressive measures, as well as a plan for a limited experiment in **COMMUNITY RADIO**.

Pressure from the **Community Radio Association** had also convinced the government, which announced the conditions for 21 licences in July 1985.

After 266 applications had been received, the government delayed and then abruptly cancelled the experiment, fearful, perhaps, of the electoral consequences of freedom of speech. It remains to be seen whether new waves of **piracy** will emerge.

IN MANY AREAS OF THE WORLD, RADIO IS BEING USED AS PART OF ARMED STRUGGLE.

In **EL SALVADOR**, for example, the **FMLN's RADIO VENCEREMOS** operates literally underground, moving with the guerillas under bombardment. Switching frequencies to avoid the jamming by US warships, it is nevertheless listened to by the population and even by the government troops who learn more about their own casualties from Venceremos than from their own superiors.

The Farabundo Martí National Liberation Front (FMLN), the umbrella organisation which tries to organise the five guerrilla factions fighting in El Salvador, has Radio Venceremos. 'Listen to the radio. You hear the truth on the radio,' a citizen of Dulce de Nombre de María told me when I asked him about the bombing at El Ocotal.

THE BUMPER BOOK OF DIRTY TRICKS

THIS IS VENCERE-GLUG!

VENCEREMOS AÚN !!

GUATEMALA   EL SALVADOR   HONDURAS   NICARAGUA   COSTA RICA   PANAMA

[180]

Following the invasion of **EAST TIMOR** by **INDONESIAN** troops in 1975, **FRETILIN** guerillas took to the hills and operated **RADIO MAUBERE**, using US-made WW2 equipment left behind by the Portuguese after their withdrawal from the colony earlier that year. The broadcasts were picked up by neighbouring **AUSTRALIA** on the Northern Territories Outpost Radio system until November 1976. Despite the deaths of five Australian TV journalists during pre-invasion incursions —and the later disappearance of another on his way to the **MARCONI** Centre to report the invasion — the Australian government instructed Telecom officials not to pass on messages from East Timor. The arrest of a Fretilin representative in Darwin and the confiscation of his transmitter effectively shut down Fretilin's link with the outside world — except for their scoring a glorious propaganda coup in 1980 when they blew up the Indonesian TV transmitter inaugurated by President Suharto in East Timor two years earlier.

What has this kind of broadcasting got to do with the non-profit local radio – autonomous and separate from state and commercial systems – which is allowed to operate at the margins of media systems in countries such as the USA, Canada and Australia?

There is a connection. Community radio is a vital channel for the articulation of dissent and the propagation of those alternative ideas which the mainstream media systematically ignore or distort. In the words of the MacBride Report (UNESCO, 1980), 'communication nowadays is a matter of human rights', and support for human rights is the essence of community radio whether in Poland, Afghanistan, London, the Caribbean or Central America.

What is to be done?

IT IS difficult to make a specific set of proposals when the damage done by Reaganomics and Thatcherism has still to be counted. We may even need to invoke state power to re-regulate a market where 'freedom' has meant the invasion of multinational capital and the privatisation of public services.

REGULATION is needed to *protect* diversity. It need not entail the dead hand of bureaucratic, centralised control, moralising censorship, or political propaganda. *Some* public intervention is necessary, working at a distance from government itself, to encourage sectional and local cultural initiatives and to create the space for alternative forms of ownership and control.

NATIONAL and local programming needs protection by quotas that limit the amount of foreign and non-local material broadcast. Cross-subsidy on the Channel 4-model (where ITV profits pay for C4) would enable the profits from one sector to support minority, local or experimental programming.

WE NEED to develop new methods of ascertaining audience needs. It's impossible to make changes when audience research merely shows that people like what they are getting already. How do we know whether we'd like something if it has never been on the menu? The answer is to create a structure which favours programme experiment, and backs it with careful action research.

ACCOUNTABILITY in broadcasting should be improved. This means acknowledging a right to information (preferably within a Freedom of Information Act) which would enable us to make a comparison between what broadcasters promise or are obliged to deliver and what they actually do.

I T ALSO means that we should be able to press for sanctions against stations that fail to deliver. At present this is impossible. The BBC, despite its cloud of advisory committees, is not really accountable except at the distant level of Parliament. On the commercial side, the franchise contract is between the IBA and a company – legally the public has no standing. In the USA, however, any member of the public can bring a 'petition to deny' a franchise at the time it comes up for renewal. We also need information about ownership in order to control take-overs in the commercial sector.

P ERHAPS, as Brecht said, these changes can only be fully brought about in a different social system from the one we have now. But although broadcasting institutions are part of the structures of power, that doesn't mean it's a waste of time to campaign for change. On the contrary, our efforts to bring an end to the suicidal dependence on nuclear arms and nuclear energy, to stop sexist, racist and imperialist oppression and to share and use the world's natural resources more fairly and effectively, must attend to communications as well.

W E should begin by putting our own house in order, for it's in the rich countries of the North that the capital and technology, tradition and practice exported to other parts of the world have become restrictive and undemocratic.

Going Further

For broadcasting history, *Power Without Responsibility* (James Curran and Jean Seaton, Methuen, 1985) is good on the early BBC, and Erik Barnouw's *The Tube of Plenty* (OUP, 1975) takes the USA's story up to modern times. Stuart Hood's *On Television* (Pluto, 1983) is a radical critique of broadcasting by someone who has held top posts in both BBC and ITV.

Really Bad News (Writer & Readers, 1982) is the most recent of the Glasgow University Media Group's analyses of TV news coverage. *It Ain't Half Racist, Mum* (ed. Phil Cohen and Carl Gardner, Comedia, 1982) concentrates on racist aspects of news and representation. *Television Mythologies* (ed. Len Masterman, Comedia No. 24) contains a number of readable essays which illustrate the technique of 'decoding' a programme's meaning. *The World Wired Up* (Brian Murphy, Comedia, 1983) and *International Image Markets* (Armand Mattelart et al, Comedia, 1984) help make sense of global patterns of communication. *Bending Reality* (ed. James Curran et al, Pluto with Campaign for Press and Broadcasting Freedom, 1986) offers a range of critical essays and strategies for media reform from a Left perspective which unfortunately neglects radio. *Relay* magazine (quarterly from 9 Wickham Road, London SE4 1PF) has covered radical radio discussion and practice in Britain and overseas since 1981.

Useful organisations are:

The Campaign for Press and Broadcasting Freedom, 9 Poland Street, London W1V 3DG, which has strong trade union affiliations and operates a Women's Group.

Community Radio Association, 13 Midland Road, St. Philips, Bristol BS2 0JT.

The Television Users' Group, 29 Old Compton Street, London W1V 5PL.

Women's Airwaves, 12 Middle Row, London W10.

Black Women in the Media, c/o *Outwrite*, Oxford House, Derbyshire Street, London E2.

NOTES ON ILLUSTRATIONS

COLLECTIONS AT THE SCIENCE MUSEUM, BRITISH TELECOM TECHNOLOGY SHOWCASE (135 QUEEN VICTORIA ST., EC4) AND IBA BROADCASTING GALLERY (70 BROMPTON ROAD, SW3) HAVE BEEN VERY USEFUL FOR THE HISTORY OF TELEGRAPHY AND BROADCASTING.

WHILE ILLUSTRATIONS HAVE BEEN BASED ON A WIDE VARIETY OF SOURCES, IN PARTICULAR WE WOULD LIKE TO ACKNOWLEDGE THE USE OF PICTURES FROM: INSTITUTION OF ELECTRICAL ENGINEERS, P.12; SCIENCE MUSEUM, P.15; BRITISH TELECOM TECHNOLOGY SHOWCASE, P.19; CABLE & WIRELESS, P.20; SCIENTIFIC AMERICAN, P.22; DE NATUUR, P.23; THE BROADCASTER, P.49; THE ILLUSTRATED LONDON NEWS, PP.42-3; POSTERS OF PROTEST AND REVOLUTION, PP.58,105 & 171 (ADAMS & DART, 1970); THE MARCONI CO. LTD., P.63; ROBIDA (BETTMAN ARCHIVE), P.85; POPULAR TELEVISION (PITMAN 1935), TITLE PAGE, PP.92 TOP AND BOTTOM, 93 BOTTOM; LIBRARY OF CONGRESS, P.92 MIDDLE; TRANSWORLD FEATURE SYNDICATE INC., P.104, MAIN PICTURE; JEAN REY / HOLMÉS-LEBEL, PARIS, P.105, BOTTOM.

ELSEWHERE, DRAWINGS HAVE BEEN BASED ON PHOTOGRAPHS FROM THE MARCONI CO. LTD, PP. 32-48; A HISTORY OF THE CINEMA BY ERIC RHODE (ALLEN LANE, 1976), P.51; LIBRARY OF CONGRESS, P.61, BOTTOM; BBC YEAR BOOKS, PP. 79-80.

OTHER USEFUL SOURCES OF ILLUSTRATION HAVE BEEN EARLY ISSUES OF BROADCASTING MAGAZINES SUCH AS AMATEUR WIRELESS, WIRELESS WORLD AND PRACTICAL TELEVISION. SOME OF THE GRAPHICS IN CHAPTER 2 HAVE BEEN TAKEN OR ADAPTED FROM ISSUES OF SCIENCE AND INVENTION (USA) AND MODERN WIRELESS (UK). OTHER HELPFUL PUBLICATIONS ARE AS FOLLOWS:

MARCONI BY W.P. JOLLY (CONSTABLE, 1972); MY FATHER MARCONI, BY DEGNA MARCONI (FREDERICK MULLER, 1962); LOOKING AT HISTORY BY R.J. UNSTEAD (A & C BLACK, 1955); NELSON BY FRANK HUMPHRIS (LADYBIRD BOOKS, 1980); UNDERSTANDING TELECOMMUNICATIONS BY MICHAEL OVERMAN (LUTTERWORTH PRESS, 1974); THE INVENTIONS THAT CHANGED THE WORLD (READERS' DIGEST, 1982); HISTORY OF THE 20TH CENTURY (BPC PUBLISHING LTD 1969); THOSE RADIO TIMES BY SUSAN BRIGGS (WEIDENFELD & NICOLSON, 1981); TELECOMMUNICATIONS BY ERYL DAVIES (HMSO); INFORMATION REVOLUTION BY LYNN MYRING AND IAN GRAHAM (USBORNE, 1983); GUNS

AT SEA BY PETER PADFIELD (HUGH
EVELYN, 1973); THE BRITISH CB
BOOK BY PETER CHIPPINDALE
(KONA PUBNS. LTD. 1981); THE
UK CB HANDBOOK BY ALAN
AINSLIE (BUTTERWORTH & CO.,
1982); TELEVISION BY MICHAEL
LOFTUS (HAMLYN 1979); TELE-
VISION BY KEITH WICKS (MAC-
DONALD & CO. 1975); TELE-
VISION BY FRANCIS WHEEN...
(THAT'S ENOUGH BOOKS; WHAT
ARE YOU TRYING TO PROVE?...ED.)
(CENTURY, 1985).
THAT'S NOT QUITE IT...
THE TREATMENT OF AN ITEM
OF AGRICULTURAL NEWS IN THE
FICTIONAL`STORY OF SOUTHIA'
(CHAPTER 4) IS BASED ON AN
ARTICLE BY IVOR GABER IN
MULTI-CULTURAL EDUCATION.

LAST BUT NOT LEAST...
THANKS TO PHILIP, OUR EDITOR,
FOR ALL HIS HELP AND ENTHUS-
IASM, AND TO ANNE, WITH LOVE
FROM US BOTH.

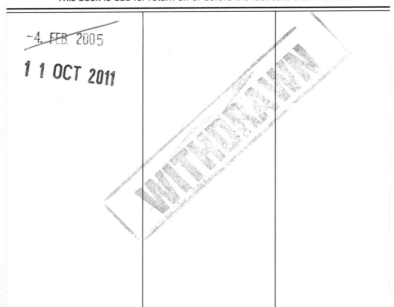
**BOOKS ARE DUE BACK ON OR BEFORE THE
ABOVE DATE**

OPENING HOURS

MON-THURS	9AM-6.30PM
FRIDAY	9AM-5PM

01708 455011 EX 2320